SINGER

Quilted Projects & Garments

Cy DeCosse Incorporated
Minnetonka, Minnesota

SINGER

SEWING REFERENCE LIBRARY®

Quilted Projects & Garments

Contents

Copyright © 1995
Cy DeCosse Incorporated
5900 Green Oak Drive
Minnetonka, Minnesota 55343
1-800-328-3895
All rights reserved
Printed in U.S.A.

QUILTED PROJECTS & GARMENTS
Created by: The Editors of Cy DeCosse
Incorporated, in cooperation with
the Sewing Education Department,
Singer Sewing Company. Singer is a
trademark of The Singer Company
Limited and is used under license.

Library of Congress
Cataloging-in-Publication Data

Quilted projects & garments.

p. cm. — (Singer sewing reference
library)
Includes index.
ISBN 0-86573-300-7
ISBN 0-86573-301-5 (pbk.)
1. Patchwork — Patterns. 2. Machine
quilting. 3. Patchwork quilts. 4. Quilted
goods. I. Cy DeCosse Incorporated.
II. Series.
TT835.Q53582 1995
746.46 — dc20   95-12392

CY DECOSSE INCORPORATED

A **COWLES** MAGAZINES COMPANY

Chairman/CEO: Bruce Barnet
Chairman Emeritus: Cy DeCosse
President/COO: Nino Tarantino
Executive V. P./Editor-in-Chief:
  William B. Jones

Also available from the publisher:
*Sewing Essentials, Sewing for the Home,
Clothing Care & Repair, Sewing for Style,
Sewing Specialty Fabrics, Sewing Activewear,
The Perfect Fit, Timesaving Sewing, More
Sewing for the Home, Tailoring, Sewing
for Children, Sewing with an Overlock,
101 Sewing Secrets, Sewing Pants That
Fit, Quilting by Machine, Decorative
Machine Stitching, Creative Sewing Ideas,
Sewing Lingerie, Sewing Projects for the
Home, Sewing with Knits, More Creative
Sewing Ideas, Quilt Projects by Machine,
Creating Fashion Accessories, Quick &
Easy Sewing Projects, Sewing for Special
Occasions, Sewing for the Holidays, Quick
& Easy Decorating Projects*

Group Executive Editor: Zoe A. Graul
Senior Technical Director: Rita C. Arndt
Technical Director: Dawn M. Anderson
Project Manager: Elaine Johnson
Associate Creative Director: Lisa Rosenthal
Art Director: Mark Jacobson
Writer: Dawn M. Anderson
Editor: Janice Cauley
Sample Production Manager: Carol Olson
Styling Director: Bobbette Destiche
Senior Technical Photo Stylist: Bridget
 Haugh
Technical Photo Stylists: Sue Jorgensen,
 Nancy Sundeen
Project Stylist: Joanne Wawra
Research Assistant: Lori Ritter
Lead Samplemaker: Phyllis Galbraith
Sewing Staff: Arlene Dohrman, Sharon
 Eklund, Valerie Hill, Kristi Kuhnau,
 Virginia Mateen, Carol Pilot, Michelle
 Skudlarek, Sue Stein, Nancy Sundeen
V. P. Development Planning & Production:
 Jim Bindas

Director of Photography: Mike Parker
Creative Photo Coordinator: Cathleen
 Shannon
Studio Manager: Marcia Chambers
Lead Photographer: Mike Parker
Photographers: Stuart Block, Rebecca
 Hawthorne, Kevin Hedden, Rex
 Irmen, William Lindner, Mark
 Macemon, Paul Najlis, Charles Nields,
 Cathleen Shannon, Greg Wallace
Contributing Photographers: Doug
 Deutscher, Paul Englund
Senior Publishing Production Manager:
 Laurie Gilbert
Senior Desktop Publishing Specialist: Joe
 Fahey
Production Staff: Amy Berndt, Deborah
 Eagle, Kevin Hedden, Jeanette Moss,
 Michelle Peterson, Mike Schauer, Greg
 Wallace, Kay Wethern, Nik Wogstad
Shop Supervisor: Phil Juntti
Scenic Carpenters: Rob Johnstone, John
 Nadeau

Quilt Consultant: Susan Stein
Consultants: Pam Hastings, Sharon
 Hultgren, Priscilla Miller, Donna
 Wilder
Contributors: American Efrid, Inc.;
 Cherrywood Quilts & Fabrics; Coats
 & Clark Inc.; Concord House,
 Division of Concord Fabrics Inc.;
 Dritz Corporation; EZ International;
 Fairfield Processing Corporation;
 Hobbs Bonded Fiber; Salem Rule;
 V.I.P. Fabrics, Division of Cranston
 Print Works Company
Printed on American paper by:
 Inland Press (0895)

Introduction

Quilted Projects & Garments includes home decorating projects and ideas for quilted clothing and accessories. This book has instructions for nine basic quilt block designs. Each of the designs appears in at least one of the projects within the book, and a sampler quilt combines all of the nine designs. Whenever possible, easy construction methods and quick cutting techniques are used. For projects that require templates, either the template pattern or the instructions for making the template are included with the project.

The Quilt Basics section shows you the basic assembly of a quilt, including selecting the fabrics and batting, as well as the techniques for cutting and piecing, quilting, basting the quilt layers together, and applying the binding. There is also helpful information on setting up your work area and on selecting equipment.

The next section of the book is Quilt Designs for the Home. This section includes instructions for the basic quilt block designs and for home decorating projects that use the designs. You can make a Pieced Heart baby quilt, a Shadowed Square pillow or lap quilt, a set of Drunkard's Path placemats, or a Nine-patch sleeping bag. The last project in this section is a sampler quilt that combines all the quilt block designs.

The final section of the book is Quilted Garments and Accessories. This section features an assortment of quilted clothing, including vests, a jacket, and a baby bunting. Also included are ideas for a tote bag and a quilted wallet-style purse.

Sampler quilt (opposite) features nine different quilt blocks.

Drunkard's Path vest (above) is made using a technique called raw edge appliqué.

Shadowed Square pillow (below) uses four shadowed square blocks to create the central diamond design.

Quilt Basics

Fabrics & Batting

Closely woven fabrics made of 100 percent cotton, including calico, muslin, and broadcloth, are the best choice for quilt tops and backings. Cotton fabric is easy to work with and is available in a wide range of colors and prints. Cotton/polyester blends may be used, but they tend to pucker when stitched.

Hand-dyed cotton fabrics in solid graduating colors are available in packets of six or eight "fat quarters," which measure about 18" (46 cm) square. These packets of fabric contain either gradations of a single color or gradations that form a bridge from one color to another. Hand-dyed fabrics are especially suitable for making quilts with subtle blends of colors or for creating a tone-on-tone effect. These hand-dyed

packets are available from quilting stores and mail-order suppliers.

Selection of the quilt backing fabric depends on the end use of the quilt. For wall hangings, where the backing fabric is not visible, an inexpensive fabric such as muslin can be used. For a lap quilt, you may want to select a solid-colored or printed fabric to coordinate with the quilt top. A solid-colored fabric accentuates the quilting stitches, while a printed fabric tends to hide them. To create added interest on the back of a quilt, the backing can be pieced, using leftover lengths of fabric from the quilt top. When seaming the backing fabric, trim away the selvages before stitching.

Rinse washable fabrics in warm water to preshrink them and remove any sizing. Check the rinse water of dark or vivid fabrics to be sure they are colorfast; if dye transfers to the water, continue rinsing the fabric until the water is clear. Machine dry the fabric until it is only slightly damp, and then press it.

Batting is available in a variety of types and is usually made of polyester, cotton, or cotton/polyester. When batting is selected for a specific project, the amount of loft in the batting, its drapability, and the distance between quilting stitches are major considerations. Follow the manufacturer's recommendations for the minimum distance between quilting stitches. This distance usually ranges from 4" to 6" (10 to 15 cm).

For quilts or quilted garments that receive heavy use, also look for a batting that resists *bearding*, the migration of fibers through the surface of the quilt. If using a batting that may beard, you can minimize the effects of bearding by selecting a tightly woven light-colored fabric for the quilt top.

Low-loft battings are recommended for machine quilting; but even low-loft battings vary in thickness. For most wall hangings or lap quilts, select a low-loft batting that is sturdy, but has some drapability. For clothing, it is usually desirable to use a thin batting that is soft and drapable, although sometimes a thick batting can give a puffy look to a garment such as a jacket. Follow the manufacturer's recommendations for pretreating the batting. Some battings must be rinsed or washed with soap before they are used.

Timesaving Cutting Techniques

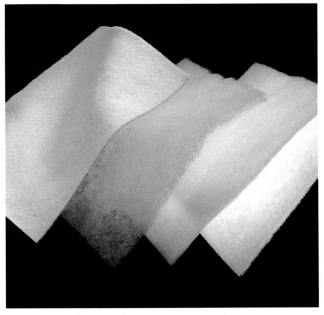

Batting is available in several types (left to right): needlepunched cotton, polyester, thin polyester designed for quilted garments, and cotton/polyester.

The projects in this book are made easily with the use of quick cutting techniques. Most pieces can be cut quickly and accurately using a rotary cutter, a cutting mat, and a clear plastic ruler. It is not necessary to straighten quilting fabrics that are off-grain or to find the grainline by pulling threads or tearing the fabric.

All pieces, including borders, sashing, and binding, are cut on the crosswise grain unless otherwise specified. Strips are cut across the width of the fabric; then the strips are cut into the required pieces. Most of the pieces can be cut using a wide, see-through quilting ruler. Tape thin strips of fine sandpaper across the bottom of see-through rulers, using double-stick tape, to prevent the ruler from slipping when you are cutting the fabric. To ensure accurate measurements for the sashing, borders, and binding, these strips are usually cut after the quilt top is completed.

Some projects in this book use a quilter's tool or template as a guide for cutting the pieces. Template patterns and instructions for making templates are included with the specific projects.

How to Cut Fabric Using Timesaving Cutting Techniques

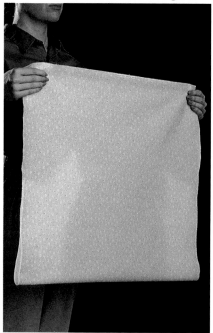

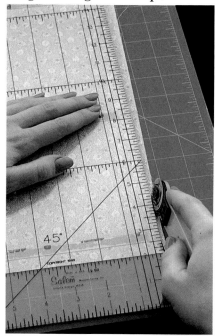

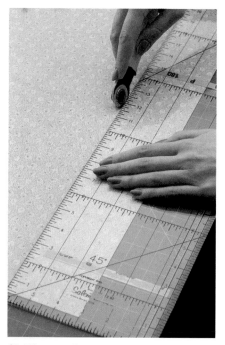

1) Fold the fabric in half, selvages together. Hold the selvage edges, letting the fold hang free. Shift one side of the fabric until fold hangs straight. Foldline is on the straight of grain.

2) Lay fabric on cutting mat, with fold along a grid line. Place ruler on fabric close to raw edge at 90° angle to fold. Trim along edge of the ruler, taking care not to move the fabric.

3) Place ruler on fabric, aligning trimmed edge with measurement on ruler; cut along edge of ruler. After cutting several strips, check fabric to be sure cut edge is still at 90° angle to fold, as in step 2.

4) Cut squares and rectangles from strips; three or four strips may be stacked with the edges matching exactly. Place the ruler on fabric near selvages at 90° angle to long edges of strips. Trim off selvages. Place ruler on fabric, aligning short edge of fabric with the measurement on ruler. Cut, holding ruler firmly.

5) Cut the squares into triangles by cutting diagonally through each square; cut once or twice diagonally, following the cutting directions for the specific project. Three or four squares may be stacked, matching the edges exactly.

Basic Piecing Techniques

The projects in this book are made using quick and easy piecing techniques and allow for ¼" (6 mm) seam allowances unless otherwise specified. Accurate stitching is critical to successful piecing. It is important to stitch seams exactly, with matching corners and points. A small error can multiply itself many times, resulting in a block or quilt that does not fit together properly. It is especially important to have accurate seam allowances on the sampler quilt (page 86) so the pieced center of the quilt fits the pieced border.

If you have a seam guide on your sewing machine, check the placement of the ¼" (6 mm) mark by stitching on a scrap of fabric. If your machine does not have a seam guide, mark one on the bed of the machine with tape. To check your stitching, measure a completed block to be sure it is the proper size. The measurement of the block should equal the desired finished size plus ½" (1.3 cm) for ¼" (6 mm) seam allowances on the sides. To achieve the correct finished block size, it may be necessary to stitch scant ¼" (6 mm) seams to allow for the turn of the cloth or shrinkage due to multiple seams.

To save time, use chainstitching whenever possible, stitching pieces together without backstitching or stopping between the pieces. Then remove the chain of units and clip the connecting threads. For secure stitching without any backstitching, stitch the pieces together using a stitch length of about 15 stitches per inch (2.5 cm). Quilt blocks composed of several units, or squares, can also be assembled using chainstitching. This method is helpful in keeping the units of a block in the proper arrangement.

When you are stitching, take care to keep the thread tensions even, and check to see that the fabric does not pucker when stitched. Match the thread color to the darker fabric, or use a neutral thread color, such as ivory, black, or gray, that will blend with all of the fabrics in the quilt.

When piecing a quilt, press the seams to one side. It is best to press them to the darker fabric to prevent show-through. Because pressing with an iron can distort bias seams, the seams are finger-pressed until a quilt block or unit has straight of grain on all four sides.

To prevent seam imprints on the right side of the quilt, press the quilt blocks or units lightly, using a steam iron. Press them first from the wrong side; then press them again from the right side. The quilt should not be pressed after it is completed, because pressing would flatten the batting.

Chainstitching is used to stitch pieced units end to end without stopping between the units.

Tips for Piecing

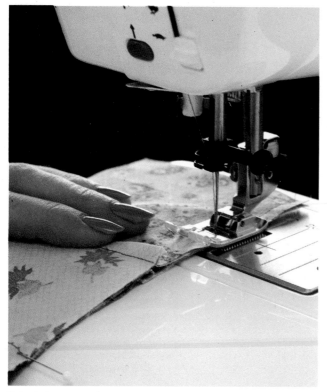

Stitch intersecting seams with the seam allowances finger-pressed in opposite directions, to distribute the bulk evenly.

Trim off any points that extend beyond the edges of a block or unit. This eliminates unnecessary bulk and allows for smooth stitching during quilting.

Pin pieces of slightly different lengths together, matching ends. Stitch with longer piece on bottom, easing in excess fullness.

Match seamlines by inserting a pin through the points where the seamlines should meet; remove the pin as you come to it.

How to Assemble a Quilt Block Using Chainstitching

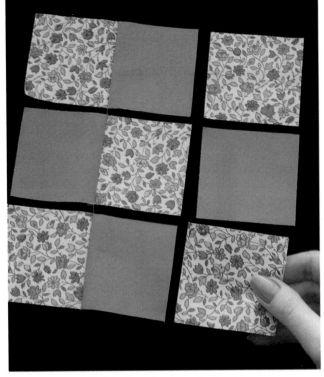

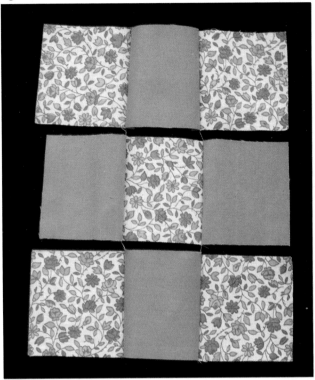

1) Arrange quilt block units into desired arrangement. Stitch first two units from top row together; do not clip thread. Repeat for next row; then continue for any remaining rows. Remove chainstitched units from machine; do not clip units apart.

2) Stitch the next unit of each row to stitched units, starting with top row. Remove chainstitched units from machine; do not clip units apart. Repeat to join any remaining units.

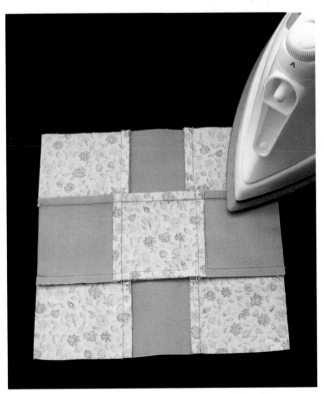

3) Stitch the rows together, finger-pressing the seam allowances in opposite directions.

4) Press long seam allowances to one side; then press the block from the right side.

Basting a Quilt

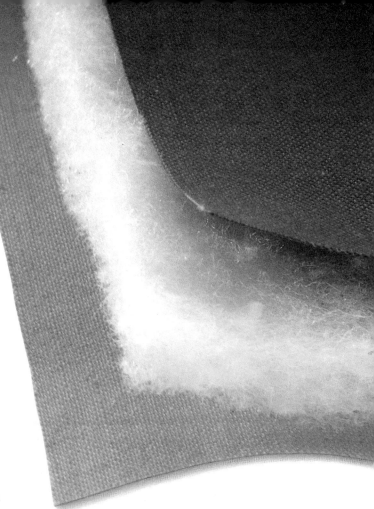

Basting is used to hold the quilt top, batting, and backing together while quilting. For ease in handling, the backing and batting should extend 2" to 4" (5 to 10 cm) beyond the edges of the quilt top on all sides.

Before layering and basting, press the quilt top and backing fabric and mark any quilting design lines. If you are using template quilting with plastic stencils, mark the quilting design lines as on page 20; it is not necessary to mark the design lines when quilting with tear-away stencils.

Follow the manufacturer's recommendations for pretreating the batting. Some battings require rinsing or washing with soap before using them. If you are using polyester batting, unroll the batting and lay it flat for several hours to allow the wrinkles to smooth out.

Traditionally, quilts were basted using a needle and thread; however, for a faster method, safety-pin basting may be used instead. Lay the quilt flat on a hard surface, such as the floor or a large table, and baste the entire quilt about every 6" (15 cm). If basting with thread, use white cotton thread and a large milliners or darning needle. Use a running stitch about 1" (2.5 cm) long. If basting with safety pins, use rustproof pins.

How to Layer and Baste a Quilt

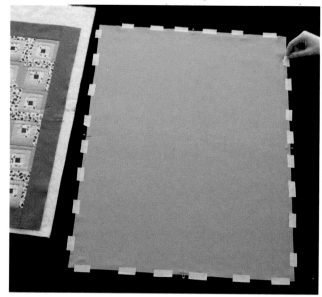

1) **Mark** center of each side of quilt top at raw edges with safety pins; repeat for batting and backing. Tape the backing, wrong side up, on work surface; begin at the center of each side and work toward the corners, stretching fabric slightly. Backing should be taut, but not stretched.

2) **Place** batting over backing, matching the pins on each side. Smooth, but do not stretch, working from center of quilt out to sides. Place quilt top right side up over the batting, matching the pins; smooth, but do not stretch.

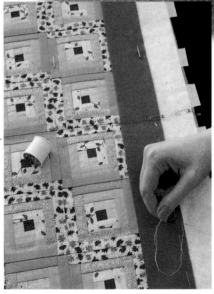

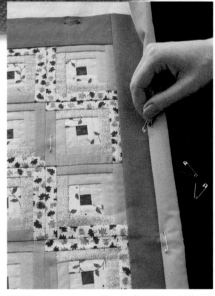

3) Baste with safety pins or thread, from the center of quilt to pins on sides; if thread-basting, pull stitches snug so the layers will not shift, and backstitch at ends. Avoid basting on marked quilting lines or through seams. (Both basting methods are shown.)

4) Baste one quarter-section with safety pins or thread, in parallel rows about 6" (15 cm) apart, working toward the raw edges. If thread-basting, also baste quarter-section in parallel rows in opposite direction. Repeat for remaining quarter-sections.

5) Remove tape from backing. Fold edges of backing over the batting and edges of quilt top to prevent raw edges of fabric from raveling and to prevent the batting from catching on needle and feed dogs during quilting. Pin-baste.

Quilting Basics

Machine quilting is used to hold the layers of the quilt together, but it also adds surface texture and depth to the quilt. A large variety of quilting designs can be created using either machine-guided or free-motion quilting or a combination of both. Plan quilting designs to cover the quilt uniformly, because heavily quilted areas tend to shrink the fabric more than lightly quilted areas.

Machine-guided Quilting

In machine-guided quilting, the feed dogs and the presser foot guide the fabric. This method of quilting is used for stitching long, straight lines or slight curves, and includes stitch-in-the-ditch quilting and channel quilting.

Stitch-in-the-ditch quilting is used to give definition to the blocks, borders, and sashing. It is the easiest method of quilting, and is often the only type of quilting needed to complete a project.

Channel quilting is the stiching of parallel lines. The quilting lines may be either diagonal, vertical, or horizontal and are usually evenly spaced. Mark the quilting lines with a straightedge.

Free-motion Quilting

In free-motion quilting, the quilt top is guided by hand, allowing you to stitch in any direction without repositioning the quilt. The feed dogs are covered or dropped for this method of quilting. Free-motion

Channel Quilting   **Stipple Quilting**   **Motif Quilting**

quilting is used to quilt designs with sharp turns and intricate curves, and includes template quilting, motif quilting, and stipple quilting.

Template quilting is used to add designs, such as motifs and continuous border designs, to a quilt. Template quilting can be done using plastic stencils or tear-away stencils. For plastic stencils, designs are transferred to the quilt top (page 20). Tear-away stencils allow you to stitch the motifs without marking the quilt top. A design, printed on translucent paper, is pinned to the basted quilt top and torn away after quilting. Free-motion stitching is generally used for template quilting; however, some designs, such as cables with gentle curves, may be quilted using machine-guided stitching.

Motif quilting is used to emphasize the printed design of a fabric and is accomplished by outlining the desired motifs. Continue stitching from one motif to the next without stopping. Although free-motion is frequently used for this type of quilting, machine-guided quilting can be used if the motifs consist of subtle curves or if the quilted project is small and can be manipulated easily under the presser foot.

Stipple quilting is used to fill in the background. It can be used to create areas of textured fabric. For uniformity throughout a project, it is best to use loose stipple quilting when combining this method with other types of quilting.

Template Quilting

Stitch-in-the-ditch Quilting

Marking the Quilting Design

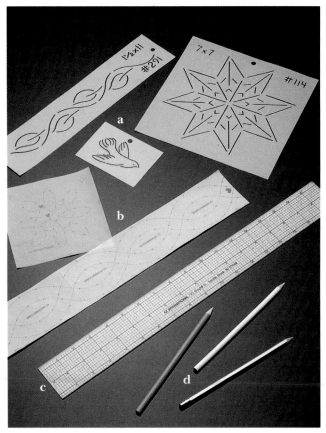

With some methods of quilting, it is necessary to mark the quilt before you begin. For channel quilting or template quilting with plastic stencils, mark the design on the quilt top before layering and basting, using a pencil or marking pencil intended for quilting. For stitch-in-the-ditch quilting, motif quilting, and stipple quilting, it is not necessary to mark the quilt top. For template quilting with tear-away stencils, the paper stencil is pinned to the quilt top after the quilt layers are basted together, eliminating the need for any additional marking.

If marking designs with pencils, test the pencils on a fabric scrap before using them on the quilt to be sure that the markings do not rub off too easily, but that they can be thoroughly brushed or erased away with a fabric eraser after quilting. Avoid using water-soluble marking pens, because the entire quilt must be rinsed thoroughly to completely remove the markings.

Marking tools and materials are helpful for marking intricate design lines. Marking tools and materials include plastic stencils **(a),** tear-away stencils **(b),** clear see-through ruler **(c),** and marking pencils **(d).**

How to Mark a Quilting Design

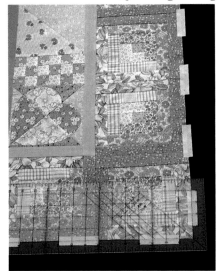

Marking pencil. 1) Press quilt top; place on hard surface, with corners squared and sides parallel. Tape securely, keeping quilt top smooth and taut.

2) Mark the quilting design, using straightedge or template as a guide, beginning at corners of quilt. Mark thin lines, using light pressure. For continuous designs, adjust length of several motifs slightly to achieve correct length.

Tear-away stencils. Press quilt top. Layer and baste quilt (pages 16 and 17). Cut stencil design, and place on quilt; secure with straight pins about 3" to 4" (7.5 to 10 cm) apart.

Quilt large projects by rolling one side of the quilt, allowing it to fit on the sewing machine bed. For even stitching, support the quilt to the left of and behind the machine.

Stitching & Handling

Cotton thread is traditionally used for quilting. Select the thread color according to how much you want the stitching to show. To avoid changing thread colors often, select one thread color that blends with all the fabrics in the quilt top. Or, to emphasize the quilting stitches and to add interest, select a contrasting or metallic thread for the quilting. Thread the machine, and loosen the needle thread tension, if necessary, so the bobbin thread does not show on the right side.

To maintain an even stitch length and to help the quilt feed through the machine evenly, do not allow the quilt to hang over the back or side of the sewing table. Set up the sewing area so the quilt will be supported both to the left of and behind the sewing machine.

Small projects are easily maneuvered as you machine-quilt. Before quilting larger projects, roll up one side of the quilt to allow it to fit on the sewing machine

bed. If the sewing surface is not large enough to hold the remaining width, roll up both sides of the quilt.

Plan the sequence of the quilting before you begin to stitch. Begin by anchoring the quilt horizontally and vertically by stitching in the ditch of a seamline near the center and then stitching along any borders; this prevents the layers from shifting. Next, stitch along any sashing strips or between blocks. Once the quilt has been anchored into sections, quilt the areas within the blocks and borders.

Stitch continuously, with as few starts and stops as possible. Prevent tucks from being stitched in the backing fabric by feeling through the layers of the quilt ahead of the sewing machine needle and continuously easing in any excess fabric before it reaches the needle. If a tuck does occur, release the stitches for 3" (7.5 cm) or more and restitch, easing in excess fabric.

Quilting Techniques

For machine-guided quilting, such as stitch-in-the-ditch and channel quilting, it is helpful to stitch with an Even Feed® foot, or walking foot, if one is available; this type of presser foot helps to prevent puckering. Position your hands on either side of the presser foot and hold the fabric taut to prevent the layers from shifting. Stitch, using a stitch length of 10 to 12 stitches per inch (2.5 cm), and ease any excess fabric under the foot as you stitch. The presser foot and feed dogs guide the quilt through the machine.

For free-motion quilting, such as template, motif, and stipple quilting, remove the regular presser foot and attach a darning foot. Set the machine for a straight stitch, and use a straight-stitch needle plate; cover the feed dogs, or lower them. It is not necessary to adjust the stitch length setting on the machine, because the stitch length is determined by a combination of the movement of the quilt and the speed of the needle. Use your hands to guide the fabric as you stitch, applying gentle tension. With the presser foot lifter in the lowered position, stitch, moving the fabric with wrist and hand movements. Maintain a steady rhythm and speed as you stitch, to keep the stitch length uniform. When changing your hand positions, stop stitching, with the needle down in the fabric.

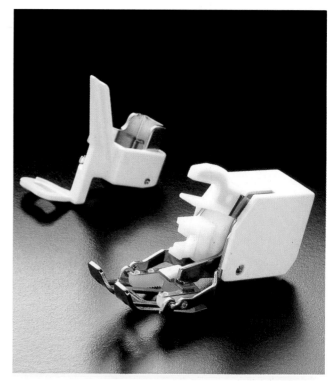

Presser feet recommended for quilting include the darning foot (left) and the Even-Feed or walking foot (right). An Even-Feed foot is used for machine-guided quilting. A darning foot is used for free-motion quilting.

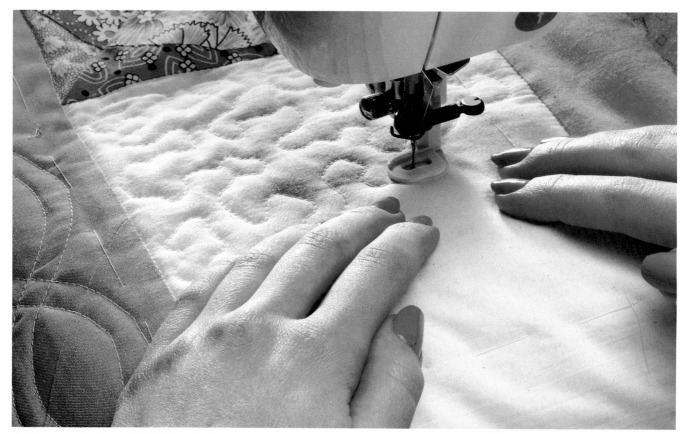

Quilting techniques, including both free-motion and machine-guided, are used to add dimension to a quilt.

How to Secure the Thread Tails

1) Draw up the bobbin thread to the quilt top, by turning flywheel by hand and stopping with needle at highest position. Pull on needle thread to bring the bobbin thread up through the fabric.

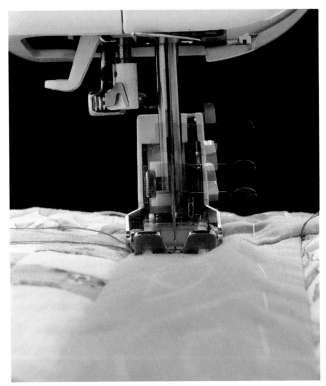

2) Stitch several short stitches to secure threads at the beginning of stitching line, gradually increasing stitch length for about ½" (1.3 cm), until it is desired length. Reverse procedure at end of stitching.

How to Quilt Using Machine-guided and Free-motion Techniques

Stitch-in-the-ditch quilting. Stitch over the seamline, stitching in the well of the seam.

Channel quilting. Stitch parallel quilting lines, starting with inner marked line and working outward.

(Continued on next page)

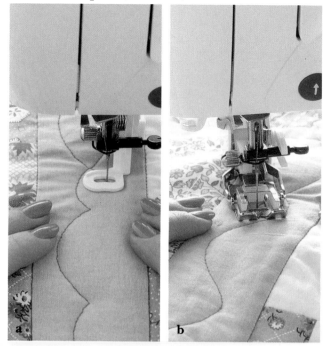

Single-motif template quilting with plastic stencils. Mark design, using marking pencil and plastic stencil (page 20). Stitch as much of design as possible in long, continuous lines, without stopping.

Continuous-motif template quilting with plastic stencils. Mark design, using marking pencil and stencil (page 20). Stitch motifs along one side to points where motifs connect **(a)**. Or stitch one side of first motif, then opposite side of second motif, and repeat **(b)**. Return to starting point; stitch motifs on opposite side.

Template quilting with tear-away stencils. Stitch either single motif or continuous motif, following the directional arrows on paper stencil. Tear away the paper stencil.

Stipple quilting. Stitch random, curving lines, beginning and ending at an edge and covering background evenly. Work in small sections; keep spaces between quilting lines close. Do not cross over lines.

Motif quilting. Determine longest continuous stitching line possible around desired motif. Stitch around motif without stopping; continue to next motif. Stitch any additional design lines as necessary.

Binding a Quilt

Double binding provides durable finished edges for quilts. The binding can be cut to match the border of the quilt, or it can be cut from a fabric that coordinates with the pieced quilt top.

Double binding, cut on the straight of grain, has two popular finished widths. Regular binding has a finished width of a scant ½" (1.3 cm), and narrow binding has a finished width of a scant ⅜" (1 cm). Regular binding is used for most quilts; cut the binding strips 2½" (6.5 cm) wide. Narrow binding is used for small quilts, such as wall hangings that are 36" (91.5 cm) or smaller; cut the binding strips 2" (5 cm) wide.

The directions for each quilt in this book specify either regular or narrow binding, and the required binding yardage is given. Binding strips are cut on the crosswise grain of the fabric and pieced to the necessary length.

How to Bind a Quilt with Double Binding

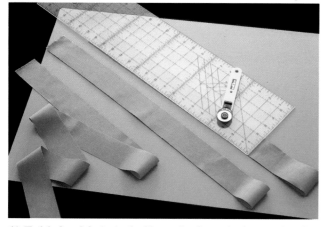

1) **Fold** the fabric in half on the lengthwise grain. On the crosswise grain, cut strips 2½" (6.5 cm) wide for regular binding or 2" (5 cm) wide for narrow binding.

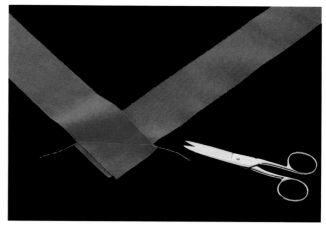

2) **Pin** strips, right sides together, at right angles, if it is necessary to piece binding strips; strips will form a V. Stitch diagonally across strips.

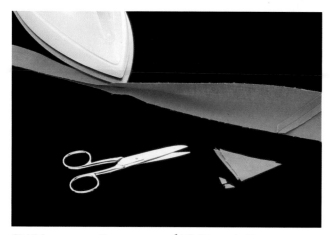

3) **Trim** seam allowances to ¼" (6 mm). Press seam open. Trim points even with edges. Press the binding strip in half lengthwise, wrong sides together.

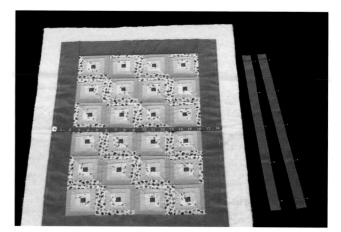

4) **Measure** quilt top across middle. Cut two binding strips equal to this measurement plus 2" (5 cm). Mark binding strips 1" (2.5 cm) from ends; divide area between pins in fourths, and pin-mark. Divide upper and lower edges of quilt in fourths; pin-mark.

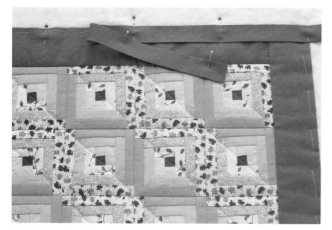

5) **Place** the binding strip on upper edge of quilt top, matching the raw edges and pin marks; binding will extend 1" (2.5 cm) beyond quilt top at each end. Pin binding along length, easing in any fullness.

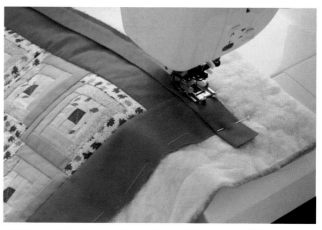

6) **Stitch** binding strip to the quilt, a scant ¼" (6 mm) from raw edges of binding.

7) Trim the excess batting and backing to a scant ½" (1.3 cm) from stitching for regular binding; trim to a scant ⅜" (1 cm) for narrow binding.

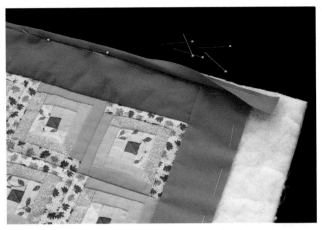

8) Wrap binding strip snugly around edge of quilt, covering stitching line on back of quilt; pin in the ditch of the seam.

9) Stitch in the ditch on right side of quilt, catching binding on back of quilt.

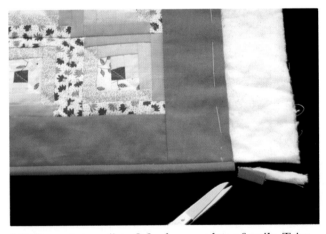

10) Repeat steps 5 to 9 for lower edge of quilt. Trim ends of upper and lower binding strips even with the edges of quilt top.

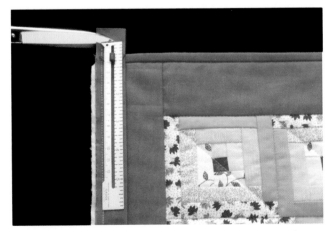

11) Repeat steps 4 to 7 for sides of quilt, measuring the quilt top down middle in step 4. Trim the ends of binding strips to extend ½" (1.3 cm) beyond the finished edges of quilt.

12) Fold binding along the stitching line. Fold ½" (1.3 cm) end of binding over finished edge; press in place. Wrap binding around edge, and stitch in the ditch as in steps 8 and 9. Slipstitch end.

Quilt Designs
for the Home

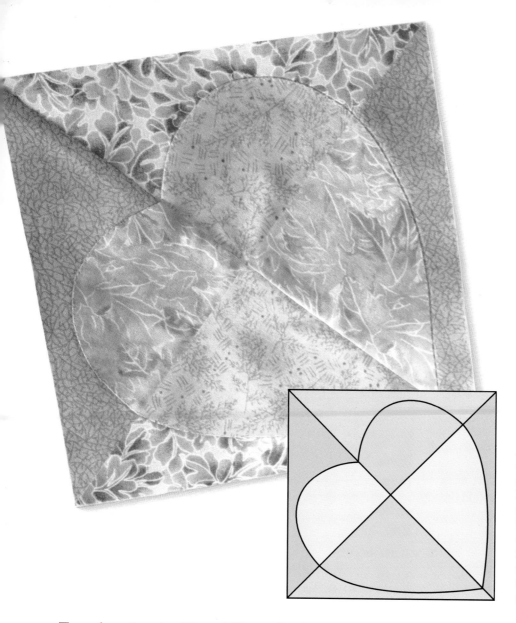

Pieced Heart Design

The quick piecing technique used to make the Pieced Heart quilt block actually yields two blocks. Two hearts are appliquéd to two background squares. Then the squares are cut and reassembled to make two 6" (15 cm) finished Pieced Heart blocks. Select two fabrics for the heart and two background fabrics that contrast.

A template made from cardboard or template material is used for shaping the heart appliqués. The hearts are applied to the background squares, using a technique called blindstitch appliqué (pages 44 and 45). For stitching that is almost invisible, use monofilament nylon thread in the needle and thread that matches the backing fabric in the bobbin.

Template for the Pieced Heart Design

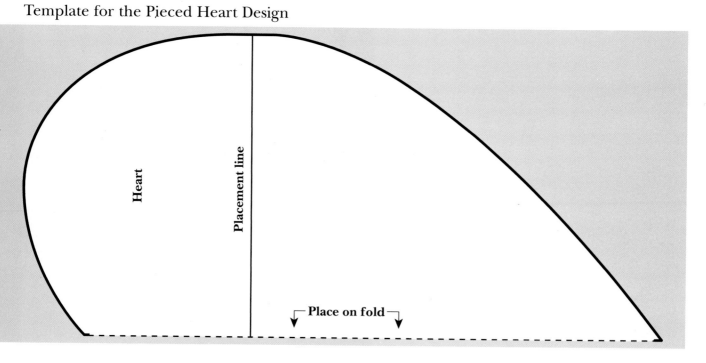

Heart

Placement line

⌐ **Place on fold** ⌐

How to Sew a Pieced Heart Block

1) Cut one 7¼" (18.7 cm) square each from two background fabrics.

2) Trace template (opposite) onto paper. Fold paper on dotted line; cut on outer solid line. Trace heart onto cardboard; transfer placement line to template. Cut out template.

3) Place template on heart fabric on the straight of grain. Adding ¼" (6 mm) seam allowance, cut around heart. Clip inside corner almost to template. Repeat to cut remaining heart from second fabric.

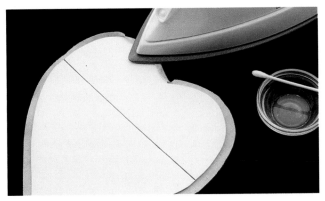

4) Spray starch in small bowl; dab starch on section of seam allowance. Place template on wrong side of heart. With tip of iron, press seam allowance over edge of template; using dry iron, press until spray starch dries. Continue pressing around heart. Turn heart over; press right side up.

5) Mark each side of heart appliqué at the placement line, on seam allowance, using marking pencil. Fold background square diagonally in both directions; press foldlines. Center heart diagonally on square, aligning placement marks with a foldline; pin in place. Repeat for remaining heart and background square.

6) Position tear-away stabilizer, cut larger than heart, on wrong side of background square. Appliqué the hearts to squares as on page 45, step 5. Remove stabilizer. Cut squares diagonally in both directions.

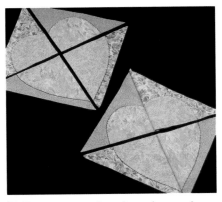

7) Rearrange triangles, alternating fabrics to make heart blocks. Using ¼" (6 mm) seams, stitch the upper heart triangles, right sides together; then stitch lower heart triangles together.

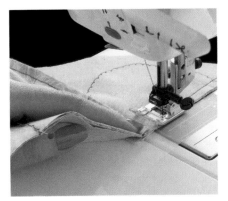

8) Stitch upper portion of heart to lower portion of heart, matching raw edges and finger-pressing seam allowances in opposite directions. Press block, pressing long seam allowances to one side.

Pieced Heart Quilts

This Pieced Heart quilt, used as a wall hanging or baby quilt, makes the perfect gift. Created from the Pieced Heart design (page 30), the finished quilt measures about 34" × 50" (86.5 × 127 cm). The quilt consists of fifteen heart blocks separated by sashing strips with connecting squares. To create a lasting memento of a special occasion, such as an anniversary, reunion, bridal or baby shower, make a friendship quilt by having family members or friends sign the quilt along the sashing strips.

The pieces of the heart blocks are assembled to make two styles of blocks. The Pieced Heart baby quilt opposite has blocks of various colors. Each block is made from two heart fabrics and two background fabrics. The blocks for the Pieced Heart wall hanging above are made using four fabrics for the hearts and two fabrics for the background.

For a friendship quilt, the signatures may be obtained before or after the quilt top is stitched together. Use a permanent-ink marking pen for the signatures, testing the pen by writing on a scrap of the sashing fabric and washing the fabric several times to see if the ink bleeds or fades. If you are collecting signatures on the sashing strips before the quilt top is assembled, prevent the fabric from slipping during signing by placing the strips on a piece of fine-grit sandpaper or

taping them to a piece of cardboard. You may also want to record on a sashing strip who the signers are, when the quilt was made, and if it was made for a special occasion.

✂ Cutting Directions

From each background fabric, cut two 7¼" (18.7 cm) strips; from the strips, cut eight 7¼" (18.7 cm) background squares of each fabric.

Make the heart template and cut sixteen hearts as on page 31, steps 2 and 3. For the baby quilt, cut two hearts from each of the eight heart fabrics; for the wall hanging, cut four hearts from each of the four heart fabrics.

Cut seven 2½" (6.5 cm) strips from sashing fabric; these will be cut to size for the sashing strips on page 34, step 4. Cut twenty-four 2½" (6.5 cm) squares from the heart fabrics; these will be used for the connecting squares in the sashing.

Cut four 4½" (11.5 cm) strips from the border fabric; these will be cut to size for the border strips on page 35, step 9. Cut four 4½" (11.5 cm) squares from one or more heart fabrics, to use for the corner squares of the border. Cut five 2½" (6.5 cm) strips from the binding fabric.

YOU WILL NEED

For a wall hanging:

⅜ yd. (0.35 m) each of four fabrics, for hearts, connecting squares of sashing, and corner squares of border.

½ yd. (0.5 m) each of two fabrics, for background.

⅝ yd. (0.6 m) fabric, for sashing.

⅝ yd. (0.6 m) fabric, for border.

1½ yd. (1.4 m) fabric, for backing.

⅜ yd. (0.35 m) fabric, for binding.

Batting, about 38" × 54" (96.5 × 137 cm).

⅓ yd. (0.32 m) muslin, for fabric sleeve, to hang quilt.

Lattice, for hanging quilt.

For a baby quilt:

¼ yd. (0.25 m) each of eight fabrics, for hearts, connecting squares of sashing, and corner squares of border.

½ yd. (0.5 m) each of two fabrics, for background.

⅝ yd. (0.6 m) fabric, for sashing.

⅝ yd. (0.6 m) fabric, for border.

1½ yd. (1.4 m) fabric, for backing.

⅜ yd. (0.35 m) fabric, for binding.

Batting, about 38" × 54" (96.5 × 137 cm).

Pieced Heart design, used in an autographed wall hanging (opposite) or a pastel baby quilt (below), makes a perfect gift.

How to Sew a Pieced Heart Baby Quilt

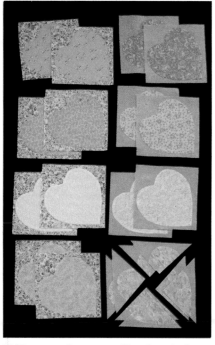

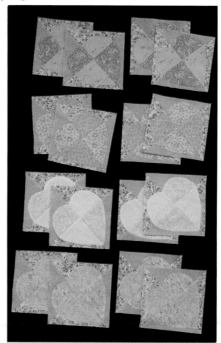

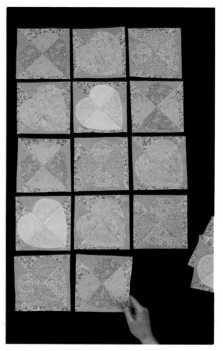

1) Prepare heart appliqués, stitch to background squares, and cut as on page 31, steps 3 to 6; stitch hearts from four fabrics to squares of one background fabric. Stitch hearts of remaining fabrics to squares of second background fabric.

2) Reassemble the triangles as on page 31, steps 7 and 8, to make 16 blocks as shown.

3) Arrange blocks as desired into five rows of three blocks; there is one extra block that will not be used for the quilt.

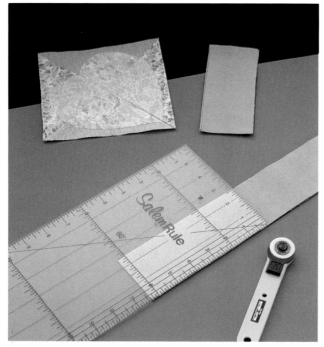

4) Measure sides of several quilt blocks to determine the shortest measurement; from the 2½" (6.5 cm) sashing strips, cut 38 strips to this length.

5) Stitch the sashing strips between blocks, right sides together, to form rows. Stitch strips to ends of rows. Press seam allowances toward sashing strips.

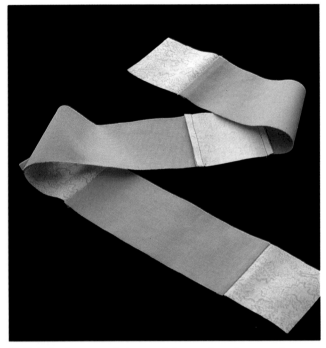

6) Stitch the remaining sashing strips alternately to the connecting squares to equal the length of the block-and-sashing row; there will be a connecting square at each end. Press seam allowances toward sashing strips.

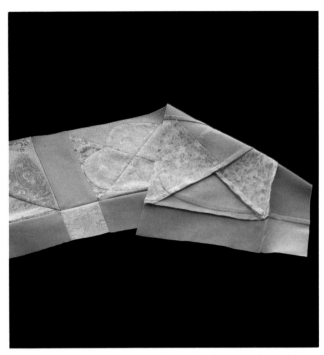

7) Place one sashing unit along the lower edge of first block-and-sashing row, right sides together, matching seams. Pin along length, easing in any fullness; stitch. Repeat for remaining block-and-sashing rows.

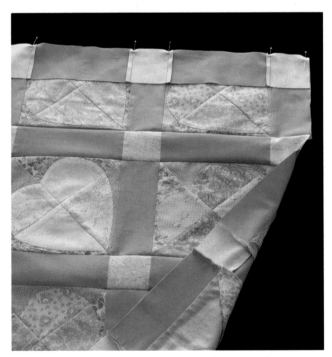

8) Pin bottom of one row to top of a second row, as in step 7; stitch. Repeat to join remaining rows. Stitch sashing unit to upper edge of first row. Press seam allowances toward sashing units.

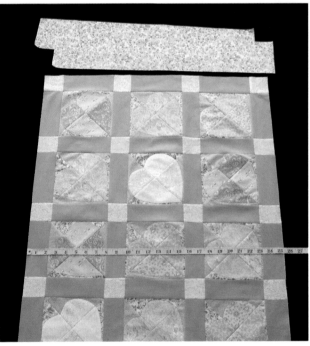

9) Measure the quilt top across the middle. From 4½" (11.5 cm) fabric strips, cut two border strips to this length. Measure the quilt top down the middle, from the top to the bottom; cut two border strips to this length.

(Continued on next page)

10) Pin upper border strip to upper edge of quilt top at center and ends, right sides together; pin along the length, easing any fullness. Stitch. Repeat at lower edge. Press seam allowances toward the border.

11) Stitch corner squares for border to ends of side border strips, right sides together. Finger-press seam allowances toward border strip.

12) Pin and stitch the pieced border strips to sides of quilt top, as in step 10, matching seamlines at corners. Press the seam allowances toward the border.

13) Cut backing fabric 4" (10 cm) wider and longer than quilt top. Layer and baste the quilt top, batting, and backing (pages 16 and 17). Quilt the wall hanging, using stitch-in-the-ditch method (pages 22 and 23). Stitch in seamlines of sashing and borders; then stitch an X through each Pieced Heart block.

14) Apply binding as on pages 25 to 27, using 2½" (6.5 cm) strips.

How to Sew a Pieced Heart Wall Hanging

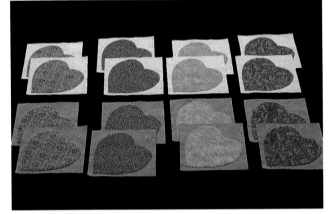

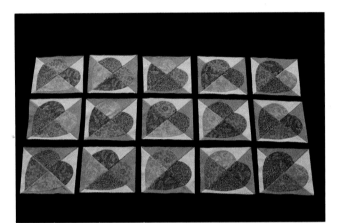

1) Prepare heart appliqués, stitch to background squares, and cut as on page 31, steps 3 to 6; stitch two hearts from each fabric to two squares of each background fabric.

2) Reassemble the triangles as on page 31, steps 7 and 8, to make 16 blocks; in step 7, alternate triangles randomly, using four heart fabrics in each block. Complete quilt as on pages 34 to 36, steps 3 to 14. Attach fabric sleeve (below).

How to Hang a Quilt Using a Fabric Sleeve

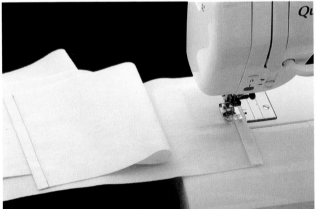

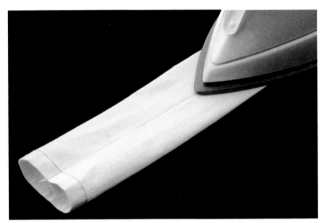

1) Cut a piece of washed, unbleached muslin 6" (15 cm) wide by the width of the quilt. Turn under and stitch ½" (1.3 cm) double-fold hems at short ends.

2) Stitch long edges of strip, right sides together, in ½" (1.3 cm) seam; press seam allowances open. Turn sleeve right side out; press flat, centering seam.

3) Pin the sleeve to the back of the quilt, close to the top edge and 1" (2.5 cm) from the ends. Hand-stitch sleeve to quilt along upper and lower edges; stitch through backing and into batting.

4) Hang the quilt by inserting strip of sealed wooden lattice, cut ½" (1.3 cm) shorter than the width of the quilt, through sleeve. Secure lattice to wall, placing screws or nails at ends of lattice.

Ohio Star Design

The Ohio Star design is created from triangles and squares, and is made from three different fabrics. Select an obvious print for the center square. For the points of the star, use a fabric that is more dominant or darker than the fabric selected for the background. Star points with too little impact will fade into the background, making the center square appear to be the only design in the quilt block. You can make a 9" (23 cm) or 12" (30.5 cm) finished block with the instructions that follow. Both block sizes are used in the sampler quilts on pages 87 and 89. A larger Ohio Star block appears in the Birthday Banner on page 40.

How to Sew an Ohio Star Block

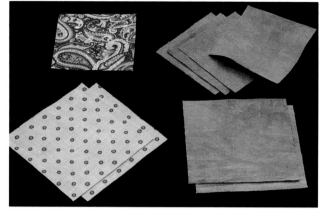

1a) For 9" (23 cm) finished block. Cut one 3½" (9 cm) square from the center square fabric and four 3½" (9 cm) squares from the background fabric. Cut two 4¼" (10.8 cm) squares each from star point fabric and background fabric.

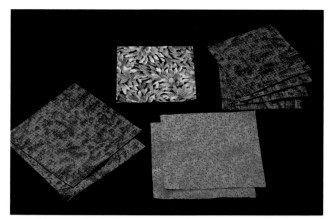

1b) For 12" (30.5 cm) finished block. Cut one 4½" (11.5 cm) square from center square fabric and four 4½" (11.5 cm) squares from background fabric. Cut two 5¼" (13.2 cm) squares each from the star point fabric and background fabric.

2) Layer the four large squares, matching raw edges; cut through squares diagonally in both directions.

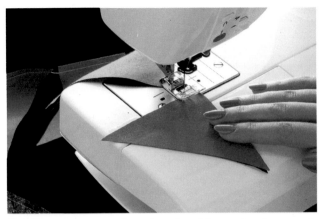

3) Align one star point triangle with one background triangle, right sides together. Stitch along one short side, taking care not to stretch bias edges; repeat for remaining units, using chainstitching (page 13).

4) Clip units apart; do not press. Place two units right sides together, alternating fabrics; finger-press seam allowances toward darker fabric. Stitch along long edge, taking care not to stretch bias edges. Repeat for remaining units, using chainstitching.

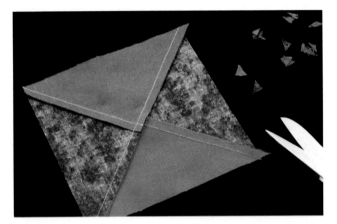

5) Clip the units apart; press the seams. Trim off the points.

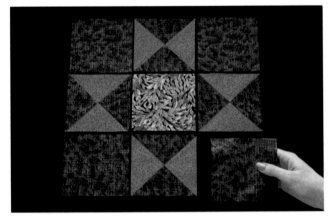

6) Arrange the units into quilt block design as shown.

7) Assemble block, using chainstitching (page 15); finger-press seam allowances toward center square. Press block.

Ohio Star Birthday Banners

This decorative wall banner features the Ohio Star design (page 38). Decorate a separate fabric square for each family member, and button it over the center of the banner to celebrate each person's birthday.

The lettering on the banner is stenciled onto the fabric before the quilt is assembled. For easy stencil designs, use the precut plastic alphabet stencils available in several sizes and styles at craft stores and office supply stores. Once stenciled, the personalized squares can be customized to each family member's interests with iron-on appliqués, embroidery, or even charms.

The finished banner measures about 31" (78.5 cm) square and hangs easily from a single nail.

✂ Cutting Directions

Cut five 8½" (21.8 cm) squares from background fabric. Cut two 9¼" (23.6 cm) squares each from star point fabric and background fabric; layer and cut the large squares as on page 39, step 2.

Cut three 4" (10 cm) strips from border fabric; trim each strip to 24½" (62.3 cm) in length for the side and lower border pieces. Cut two 1¼" (3.2 cm) strips from border fabric; trim each strip to 24½" (62.3 cm) in length for the narrow upper border pieces. The upper border piece with lettering is cut after the letters are stenciled. Cut four 4" (10 cm) squares from star point fabric for the corner squares of the border. For the binding, cut three 2" (5 cm) fabric strips.

For each personalized square, cut two 8½" (21.8 cm) squares from fabric and one 9½" (24.3 cm) square from thin batting or flannel.

Personalized fabric squares highlight interests of family members.

YOU WILL NEED

⅝ yd. (0.6 m) fabric, for background.

⅓ yd. (0.32 m) fabric, for star points and corner squares of border.

⅔ yd. (0.63 m) fabric, for border and binding.

⅛ yd. (0.15 m) light-colored fabric, for upper border with lettering.

1 yd. (0.95 m) fabric, for backing.

Plastic or tear-away paper stencil.

Batting, about 35" (89 cm) square, for banner; thin batting or flannel, 9½" (24.3 cm) square, for each personalized square.

Fabric scraps, and 6" (15 cm) length of ribbon or cording, ⅛" (3 mm) wide, for each personalized square.

Two buttons.

Embellishments, for personalized squares.

Alphabet stencil, 1¼" to 1½" (3.2 to 3.8 cm) in height; fabric paints; disposable plates; stencil brush; medium-grit sandpaper.

Sawtooth picture hanger and 29" (73.5 cm) strip of sealed wooden lattice, for hanging banner.

How to Sew an Ohio Star Birthday Banner

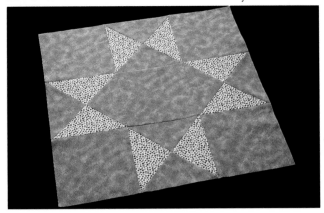

1) Assemble Ohio Star block as on page 39, steps 3 to 7; in step 6, use square from background fabric for center square of block.

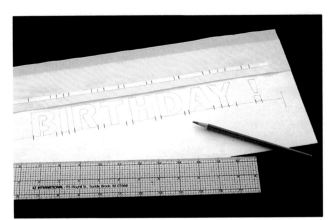

2) Determine spacing of border lettering on paper; finished length of border strip is 24" (61 cm). Mark letter spacing on a strip of tape; then position tape on fabric to use as a placement guide for letters.

(Continued on next page)

3) Place fabric, right side up, on sandpaper to keep fabric from shifting. Wrap tape around the bristles of stencil brush, ¼" (6 mm) from end. Position the first letter; apply tape to the surrounding cutout areas, if necessary to protect fabric.

4) Dip tip of stencil brush into fabric paint; blot onto folded paper towel until bristles are almost dry. Hold brush perpendicular to first letter, and apply paint, using an up-and-down motion. Repeat to stencil the remaining letters, repositioning stencil.

5) Heat-set fabric paint when it is dry, following the manufacturer's directions. Trim fabric to 2½" × 24½" (6.5 × 62.3 cm), taking care to center lettering.

6) Stitch the narrow border strips to upper and lower edges of stenciled border strip; press seam allowances toward the center.

7) Attach borders as on page 36, steps 10 to 12.

8) Cut backing fabric 4" (10 cm) wider and longer than quilt top. Layer and baste the quilt top, batting, and backing (pages 16 and 17). Quilt, using the stitch-in-the-ditch method (pages 22 and 23). Center stencil design on each corner square, and stitch, using template quilting (pages 22 and 24).

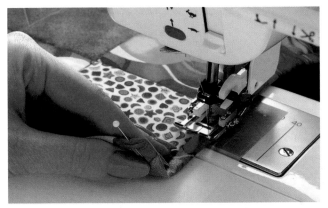

9) Apply the binding as on pages 25 to 27.

10) Embellish right side of personalized fabric square as desired with flat embellishments. Pin 3" (7.5 cm) loop of ribbon or cording to each corner as shown.

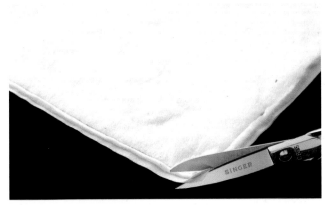

11) Place embellished square and lining right sides together; place on batting, and pin layers together. Stitch ¼" (6 mm) from all edges, leaving a 3" (7.5 cm) opening on one side. Trim batting to ⅛" (3 mm); trim corners.

12) Turn square right side out; press lightly. Slipstitch the opening closed. Attach any three-dimensional embellishments as desired. Position the personalized square over center square of banner; mark position for buttons. Stitch buttons in place.

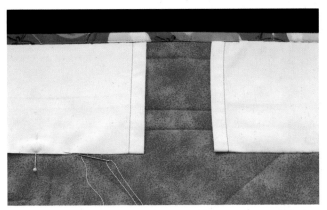

13) Cut fabric sleeve as on page 37, step 1; cut fabric strip in half to make two sleeves. Continue as on page 37, steps 1 to 3; in step 3, allow for 2" (5 cm) space at center of quilt between fabric sleeves.

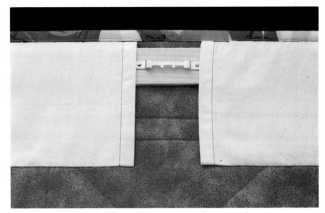

14) Insert a 29" (73.5 cm) strip of sealed wooden lattice through sleeves. Secure a sawtooth hanger to center of lattice. Hang banner from a nail.

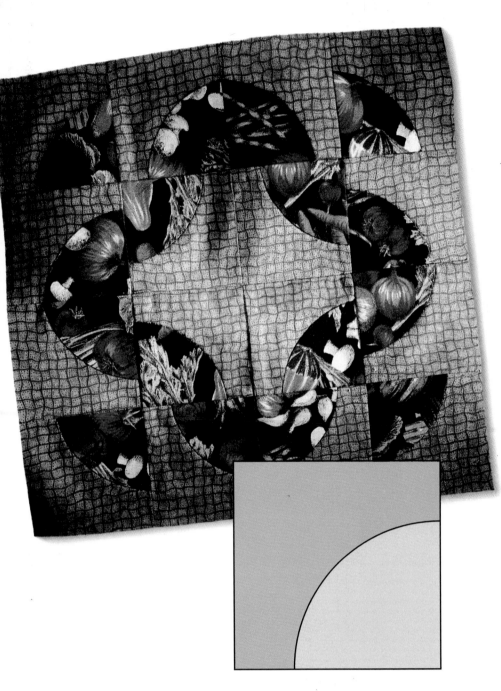

Drunkard's Path Design

The smooth, curved design of the Drunkard's Path quilt block is easily accomplished, using a technique called blindstitch appliqué. A circle appliqué, made by shaping the fabric around a cardboard template, is stitched to a background square. The square is then cut into fourths to yield four pieced Drunkard's Path units.

The Drunkard's Path quilt design shown at left is called a sixteen-patch quilt block, because it is made from sixteen units. The units can be arranged in many ways to achieve a variety of designs. The instructions that follow are for a 12" (30.5 cm) sixteen-patch block. Other designs using the sixteen-patch Drunkard's Path block appear on pages 46 and 47.

Two fabrics are needed for the Drunkard's Path quilt block. Select one fabric for the background squares and a contrasting fabric for the circles. For invisible appliqué stitching, use monofilament nylon thread in the needle and thread that matches the backing fabric in the bobbin.

How to Sew a Sixteen-patch Drunkard's Path Quilt Block

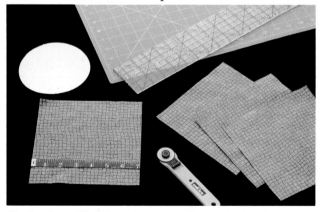

1) Cut four 7" (18 cm) squares from the background fabric. Cut a 5" (12.5 cm) circle from heavy cardboard or template material, for template.

2) Place template on contrasting fabric. Adding scant ¼" (6 mm) seam allowance, cut around the template. Repeat to cut three more circles.

3) Spray starch in a small bowl; dab starch on fabric circle, on section of seam allowance. With tip of iron, press seam allowance over edge of template; press until spray starch dries. Continue pressing around circle. Remove template, and press circle right side up. Repeat for remaining circles.

4) Center the fabric circle on the background square, matching grainlines. Position tear-away stabilizer, cut larger than circle, on wrong side of background square; pin circle in place. Repeat for remaining circles.

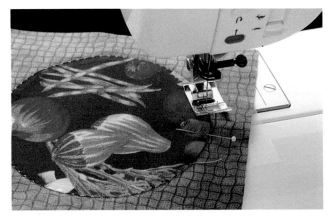

5) Set machine for short blindstitch, with the stitch width about 1/16" (1.5 mm); use monofilament thread in the needle. Blindstitch around appliqué, catching edge with widest swing of the stitch. Repeat for the remaining circles. (Contrasting thread was used to show detail.)

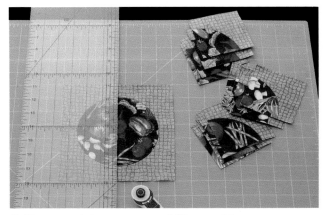

6) Remove the tear-away stabilizer, taking care not to distort the stitches. Cut through center of square in both directions to make four Drunkard's Path units. Repeat for remaining squares.

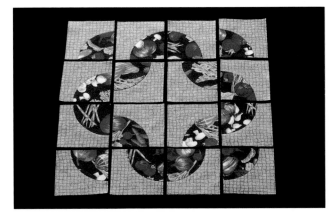

7) Arrange the 16 units as shown, or choose from other block arrangements on page 47.

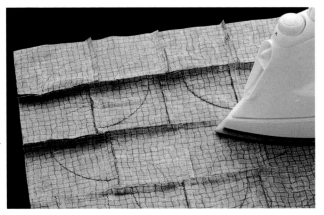

8) Assemble block, using chainstitching, as on page 15. Press block.

Drunkard's Path Placemats & Table Runners

Enhance a table with a set of quilted placemats and a table runner, using the Drunkard's Path design (page 44). For quick construction, the placemats and table runner are assembled using an easy stitch-and-turn method.

Each placemat is made from one sixteen-patch quilt block. Make all four placemats with the same sixteen-patch design, or add variety to the table setting by making each placemat with a different block design. Border strips, stitched to opposite sides of the block, are used to create a banded effect. The finished placemats measure about 12" × 18" (30.5 × 46 cm).

The table runner can be made in several lengths, depending on the number of Drunkard's Path blocks that are stitched together; a border strip is stitched to each end of the runner.

The table runner is most attractive when it is made from one block design, since the sixteen-patch block

arrangements form interesting designs when placed end to end. Experiment to see which design you like best by arranging the units in different ways before stitching the blocks. The instructions that follow are for a table runner of five sixteen-patch blocks. The finished table runner measures about 12" × 66" (30.5 × 168 cm).

✂ Cutting Directions (for four placemats)

Cut three 3½" (9 cm) strips from border fabric; cut the strips to make eight 3½" × 12½" (9 × 31.8 cm) rectangles for the border strips. Cut three 7" (18 cm) strips from background fabric; cut the strips to make sixteen 7" (18 cm) squares. Make the circle template, and cut sixteen 5" (12.5 cm) circles from fabric, as on page 44, steps 1 and 2.

Cut two 12½" (31.8 cm) strips from backing fabric; cut the strips to make eight 9½" × 12½" (24.3 × 31.8 cm) rectangles. Cut four 14½" × 20½" (36.8 × 52.3 cm) rectangles from batting.

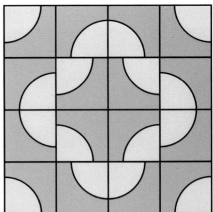

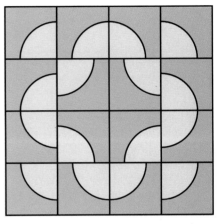

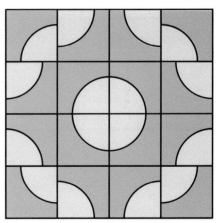

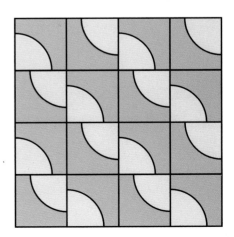

✂ Cutting Directions (for one table runner)

Cut two 3½" × 12½" (9 × 31.8 cm) rectangles from border fabric. Cut four 7" (18 cm) strips from background fabric; cut the strips to make twenty 7" (18 cm) squares. Make the circle template, and cut twenty 5" (12.5 cm) circles from fabric, as on page 44, steps 1 and 2.

Cut the backing fabric to make two 12½" × 34" (31.8 × 86.5 cm) strips. Cut one 14½" × 70" (36.8 × 178 cm) rectangle from batting.

YOU WILL NEED

For four placemats:	**For one table runner:**
⅞ yd. (0.8 m) fabric, for circles and border strips.	⅝ yd. (0.6 m) fabric, for circles and border strips.
⅔ yd. (0.63 m) fabric, for background.	⅞ yd. (0.8 m) fabric, for background.
¾ yd. (0.7 m) fabric, for backing.	¾ yd. (0.7 m) fabric, for backing.
Low-loft quilt batting.	**Low-loft quilt batting.**
Tear-away stabilizer.	**Tear-away stabilizer.**

How to Sew a Drunkard's Path Placemat

1) Make the Drunkard's Path units as on page 45, steps 3 to 6.

2) Arrange 16 units, four across and four down, in the desired block arrangement, as shown on page 47.

3) Assemble the 16-patch block, using chainstitching (page 15).

4) Stitch a border strip to each end of block. Press the seam allowances toward borders.

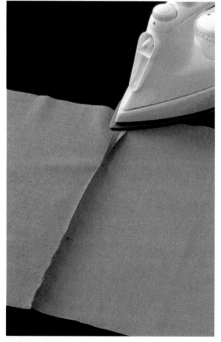

5) Place two rectangles for backing with right sides together and raw edges even; stitch ¼" (6 mm) seam on one long edge, leaving a 4" to 5" (10 to 12.5 cm) center opening for turning. Press seam open.

6) Place backing and placemat top right sides together. Center fabrics on batting, backing side up; pin or baste layers together.

7) Stitch around the placemat, ¼" (6 mm) from raw edges of fabric. Trim batting ⅛" (3 mm) from seam; trim corners diagonally.

8) Turn the placemat right side out; press lightly. Hand-stitch the opening closed.

9) Pin-baste layers together. Quilt placemat, using stitch-in-the-ditch method to define the borders and block (pages 22 and 23).

How to Sew a Drunkard's Path Table Runner

1) Follow steps 1 to 3, opposite, to make five 16-patch blocks in desired arrangement. Stitch blocks together end to end. Press seams open. Stitch a border strip to each end of the runner; press the seam allowances toward borders.

2) Follow step 5, opposite. Trim the backing to the length of the table runner top.

3) Complete the table runner as in steps 6 to 9, opposite. (Contrasting thread was used to show detail.)

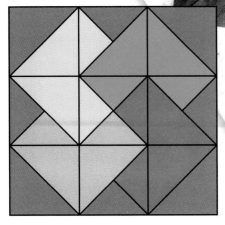

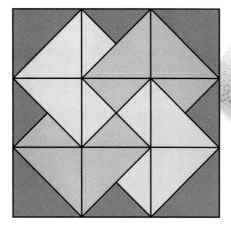

Card Trick Design

Three different pieced squares are used to make the Card Trick quilt block. The corner squares of the block are made from two triangles. The middle square on each side of the block is made from three triangles. And the center square of the block is made from four triangles. The instructions that follow are for Card Trick blocks in two sizes. The 9" (23 cm) finished

block is made using a background fabric and a different fabric for each of the four "cards." The 6" (15 cm) finished block is made using a background fabric and two card fabrics. Both block styles are used in the sampler quilt on page 87 and in the wall hanging on page 53.

How to Sew a 9" (23 cm) Card Trick Block Using Four Fabrics for the Cards

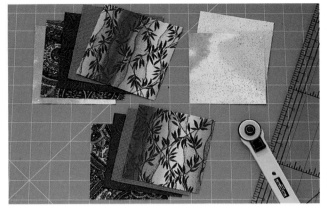

1) Cut one 4¼" (10.8 cm) square each from the background fabric and four card fabrics. Cut two 3⅞" (9.7 cm) squares from the background fabric and one from each of the four card fabrics.

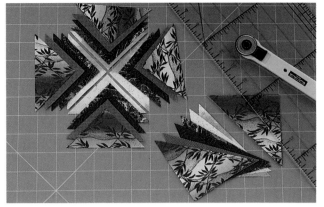

2) Cut through the large squares diagonally in both directions. Cut through the small squares diagonally in one direction.

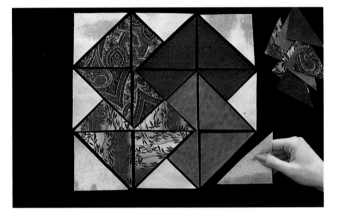

3) Arrange triangles from background and card fabrics as shown. There will be two triangles remaining from each of the four card fabrics.

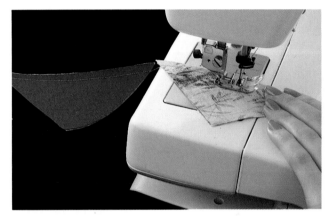

4) Stitch background and card triangles of corner square, right sides together, on long sides, using chainstitching (page 13). Repeat for remaining corner squares.

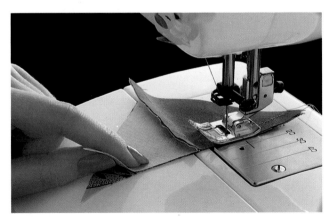

5) Make middle square for side of block by stitching small background triangle to small card triangle on one short side. Then stitch pieced triangle to the remaining triangle for the middle square, stitching right sides together on long side. Repeat for remaining middle squares.

6) Stitch two small triangles for center square of block, right sides together, along one short side. Repeat for two remaining small triangles.

(Continued on next page)

How to Sew a 9" (23 cm) Card Trick Block Using Four Fabrics for the Cards (continued)

7) Complete center square of block by stitching pieced triangle sets right sides together, on long side, finger-pressing seam allowances in opposite directions. Trim off points.

8) Assemble block, using chainstitching (page 15). Press block.

How to Sew a 6" (15 cm) Card Trick Block Using Two Fabrics for the Cards

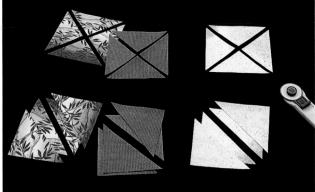

1) Cut one 3¼" (8.2 cm) square each from the background fabric and two card fabrics. Cut two 2⅞" (7.2 cm) squares each from background fabric and two card fabrics.

2) Cut through the large squares diagonally in both directions. Cut through the small squares diagonally in one direction.

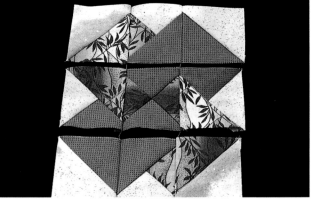

3) Arrange the triangles from the background fabric and card fabrics as shown. Assemble as on pages 51 and 52, steps 4 to 7.

4) Assemble block, using chainstitching (page 15). Press block.

Card Trick Wall Hangings

This contemporary quilt, made using the Card Trick design (page 50), incorporates two quilt block sizes. Sashing pieces, cut from a coordinating fabric, are arranged for a random look and add interest to the block arrangement.

The wall hanging is made from six 9" (23 cm) Card Trick blocks and nine 6" (15 cm) Card Trick blocks. The finished quilt measures about 33" × 51" (84 ×

129.5 cm), making it suitable for a wall hanging, baby quilt, or small lap quilt.

To add interest to the quilt, choose a narrow-striped fabric for the sashing pieces. This gives vertical and horizontal movement to the design. To unify the quilt design, you may want to use one of the card fabrics for the border of the quilt.

✂ Cutting Directions

For the 9" (23 cm) finished blocks, cut the following strips across the width of the fabric: one 4¼" (10.8 cm) strip each from the background fabric and the four card fabrics; two 3⅞" (9.7 cm) strips from the background fabric; and one 3⅞" (9.7 cm) strip each from the four card fabrics. Cut the strips to make six 4¼" (10.8 cm) squares from the background fabric, three 4¼" (10.8) squares from each of the card fabrics, twelve 3⅞" (9.7 cm) squares from the background fabric, and six 3⅞" (9.7 cm) squares from each of the card fabrics. Cut the squares diagonally as on page 51, step 2, cutting the large squares in both directions and cutting the small squares in one direction.

For the 6" (15 cm) finished blocks, cut the following strips: one 3¼" (8.2 cm) strip each from the background fabric and the four card fabrics; two 2⅞" (7.2 cm) strips from the background fabric; one 2⅞" (7.2 cm) strip each from the four card fabrics. Determine the desired arrangement of card fabrics for each of the nine 6" (15 cm) blocks. Cut strips into the necessary triangles for each block as on page 52, steps 1 and 2.

For the sashing, cut four 3½" (9 cm) strips. Cut the strips to make nine 3½" × 6½" (9 × 16.3 cm) rectangles and nine 3½" × 9½" (9 × 24.3 cm) rectangles.

For the border, cut five 3½" (9 cm) strips. The strips will be cut to size for the border strips in step 9, right. For the binding, cut four 2½" (6.5 cm) fabric strips.

YOU WILL NEED

½ yd. (0.5 m) each of four fabrics, for cards of Card Trick blocks.

⅝ yd. (0.6 m) fabric, for background of Card Trick blocks.

½ yd. (0.5 m) fabric, for sashing.

½ yd. (0.5 m) fabric, for border.

1½ yd. (1.4 m) fabric, for backing.

½ yd. (0.5 m) fabric, for binding.

Batting, about 39" × 55" (99 × 139.5 cm).

How to Sew a Card Trick Wall Hanging

1) Make six 9" (23 cm) finished Card Trick blocks as on pages 51 and 52, steps 3 to 7.

2) Make three 6" (15 cm) finished Card Trick blocks as on page 52, steps 3 and 4.

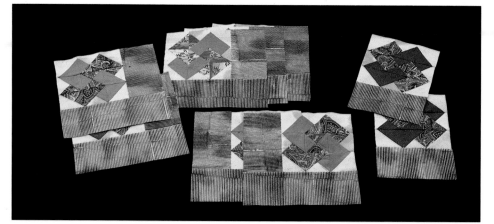

5) Stitch one long sashing strip to lower edge of one small block-and-sashing unit, right sides together; press seam allowances toward sashing strip. Repeat for six additional blocks. This gives you seven square units and two rectangular units.

8) Stitch the units together to make three rows; press seam allowances toward sashing strips. Stitch rows together; press seam allowances to one side. Press quilt top.

9) Cut and apply the border as for inner border on page 71, steps 3 to 5; consider short ends of this quilt to be upper and lower edges for this step.

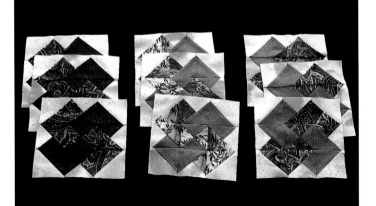

3) Repeat step 2 twice, using a different combination of card fabrics for each set of three blocks. This gives you three sets of three blocks.

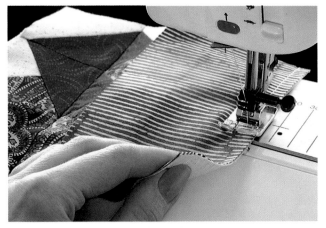

4) Stitch one short sashing strip to one side of one small block, right sides together; press seam allowances toward sashing strip. Repeat for remaining small blocks.

6) Stitch one long sashing strip to one side of one large block, right sides together; press seam allowances toward sashing strip. Repeat for a second block and long sashing strip.

7) Arrange blocks into three rows as shown. Reposition or turn blocks as necessary for pleasing overall design.

10) Cut backing fabric 4" (10 cm) wider and longer than quilt top. Layer and baste quilt top, batting, and backing (pages 16 and 17). Quilt, using stitch-in-the-ditch method (pages 22 and 23).

11) Apply binding as on pages 25 to 27.

Spools Design

The four-patch Spools quilt block consists of four spool blocks. Each spool block is made from four trapezoids and one center square. Two trapezoids become the upper and lower portions of the spool, and the remaining two trapezoids become the background in the block. The center square is cut from striped fabric to represent the thread on the spool.

For best results, cut the trapezoids for the spools and the squares for the thread from fabrics that are similar in color value. Cut the background trapezoids from a fabric that strongly contrasts with the fabrics used for the spools and thread. The trapezoids can be cut using a quilter's tool, such as the Companion Angle™, or they can be cut using the template, below.

The instructions that follow are for a 9" (23 cm) finished four-patch block. The block is used in the sampler quilts (pages 87 and 89), the Spools wall hanging (page 59), and the tote bag (page 112).

Template for the Spools Design

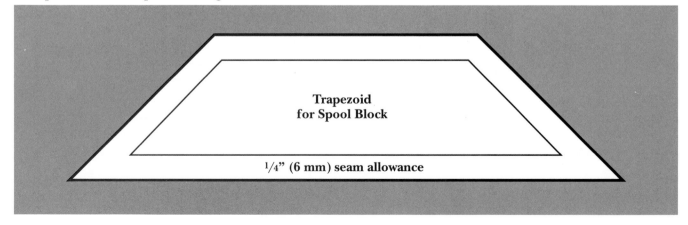

Trapezoid
for Spool Block

¹/₄" (6 mm) seam allowance

How to Sew a Four-patch Spools Block

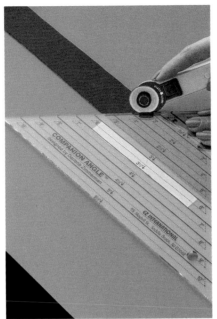

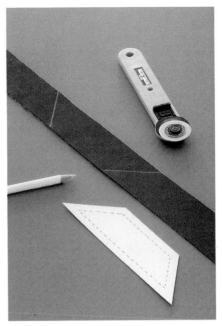

1) Cut four 3" (7.5 cm) squares from striped fabric for thread. Cut one 1½" (3.8 cm) strip each from spool fabric and background fabric; layer strips, matching raw edges.

2a) Quilter's tool. Align 5" (12.5 cm) dotted line on Companion Angle with one long side of layered strips; cut along angled edges of tool. To cut second set of trapezoids, rotate tool and align it with diagonal cut edge of fabric; cut. Repeat to cut eight trapezoids from each color.

2b) Template. Make the template (opposite) from cardboard or from template material. Align template with raw edges of fabric strips; mark along angled sides, using chalk or marking pencil. To mark second set of trapezoids, rotate and realign the tool. Repeat to mark eight sets of trapezoids. Cut on marked lines.

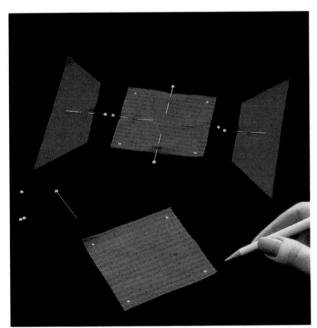

3) Mark wrong side of each thread square where the ¼" (6 mm) seams will intersect, placing a dot at each corner. Pin-mark center of each side of thread square. Pin-mark center of shortest long edge of spool and background trapezoids.

4) Align spool trapezoid to thread square, matching pin marks, with edge of trapezoid parallel to stripes of the thread square. Stitch exactly between the dots, backstitching at beginning and end of stitching. Repeat on opposite side of square.

(Continued on next page)

5) Finger-press seam allowances toward the trapezoids. Repeat step 4 to stitch the background trapezoids to the thread square.

6) Align angled ends of two adjacent trapezoids, right sides together. Stitch from the pointed end exactly to the seam intersection; backstitch. Repeat at remaining corners. Press seams of background trapezoids toward spool trapezoids and thread square; trim points.

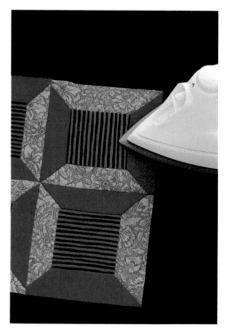

7) Continue as on pages 57 and 58, steps 3 to 6, to make four spool blocks. Stitch two blocks together, in a vertical-horizontal arrangement as shown. Finger-press seam allowances to one side.

8) Stitch remaining two squares together in a horizontal-vertical arrangement as shown. Finger-press seam allowances in opposite direction from first row.

9) Stitch the two rows together, matching seamlines. Finger-press seam allowances to one side. Press the quilt block.

Spools Wall Hangings

A decorative wall hanging, made from the Spools design (page 56), can have a country or homespun look. It may have special appeal to a person who sews. For extra detail, the border incorporates a spool block at each corner. Striped fabric is used to represent the thread on the spools. To achieve several color variations with the same striped fabric, the fabric can be overdyed, using fabric dye according to the manufacturer's instructions.

The border of the wall hanging can be embellished, if desired, with buttons of various sizes, arranged randomly. The finished wall hanging measures about 42" (107 cm) square.

✂ Cutting Directions

In the directions that follow, cut the strips across the width of the fabric. Cut ten 1½" (3.8 cm) strips from the spool fabric; cut the strips to make 80 spool trapezoids as on page 57, step 2a or 2b. Cut nine 1½" (3.8 cm) strips from the background fabric; cut the strips to make 72 background trapezoids. Cut one 1½" (3.8 cm) strip from the inner border fabric; cut the strip to make eight background trapezoids for the corner blocks of the border.

Cut three 3" (7.5 cm) strips from thread fabric; cut the strips to make 40 thread squares, each 3" × 3" (7.5 × 7.5 cm).

Cut four 2" (5 cm) strips from the inner border fabric; these will be cut to length in step 5, opposite. Cut four 5" (12.5 cm) strips from the outer border fabric;

these will be cut to length for the borders in step 6. Cut four 2½" (6.5 cm) strips from the binding fabric.

YOU WILL NEED

Striped fabric, for thread, one or more colors to total about ⅓ yd. (0.32 m).

½ yd. (0.5 m) fabric, for spools.

½ yd. (0.5 m) fabric, for background.

¼ yd. (0.25 m) fabric, for inner border and for background trapezoids of corner spool blocks.

1 yd. (0.95 m) fabric, for outer border and binding.

1½ yd. (1.4 m) fabric, for backing.

Batting, about 46" (117 cm) square.

Buttons, about 50 in various sizes and colors, optional.

How to Sew a Spools Wall Hanging

1) **Complete** nine four-patch Spools blocks as on pages 57 and 58.

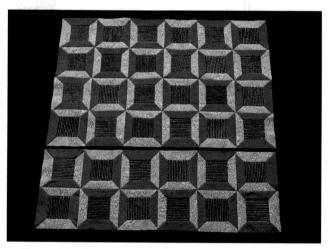

2) **Stitch** four spool blocks for border, using trapezoids cut from the inner border fabric for the background trapezoids; set aside.

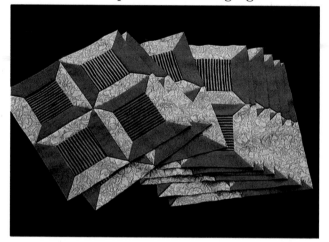

3) **Arrange** four-patch blocks as desired into three rows of three blocks.

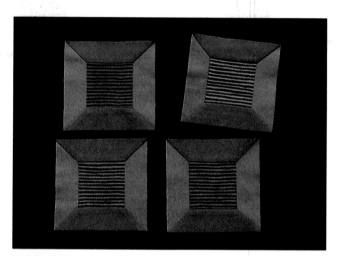

4) **Stitch** blocks into rows; then stitch rows together, finger-pressing seam allowances in opposite directions. Press quilt top.

5) Continue as on page 71, steps 3 to 5; in step 5, omit reference to piecing inner border.

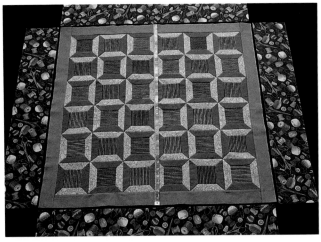

6) Measure through middle of quilt in both directions to determine the shortest measurement. Trim four 5" (12.5 cm) outer border fabric strips to this length.

7) Attach the border as on page 36, steps 10 to 12, positioning corner spools upright.

8) Cut backing fabric 4" (10 cm) wider and longer than quilt top. Layer and baste the quilt top, batting, and backing (pages 16 and 17).

9) Quilt the wall hanging, using the stitch-in-the-ditch method (pages 22 and 23). Stitch in the seamlines of inner and outer borders; then stitch between blocks and around the spools to define design. (Contrasting thread was used to show detail.)

10) Apply binding as on pages 25 to 27. Stitch buttons to border, placing buttons randomly. Attach fabric sleeve (page 37).

Shadowed Square Design

The Shadowed Square quilt block, illustrated in the graphic above right, is made from two triangles. One triangle is cut from strip-pieced fabrics and the other from a coordinating fabric. Four 6" (15 cm) blocks can be assembled to make a 12" (30.5 cm) diamond design as shown above. This design is used in the sampler quilts on pages 87 and 89 and in the pillow on page 64. The Shadowed Square block and variations of it are also used in the lap quilt on page 67.

Strip piecing, stitching fabric strips together side by side, makes interesting striped fabric from which to cut triangles. A quilter's tool, such as the Companion Angle™, can be used to cut the triangles quickly. Or, cut them using a template made from cardboard or template material. To save fabric, the tool or the template can be rotated to cut every other triangle. This produces two variations of strip-pieced triangles. For the diamond design, use four matching triangles.

How to Sew Shadowed Square Quilt Blocks

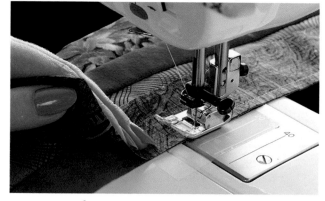

1) Cut one 1½" (3.8 cm) strip across the width of five different fabrics. Stitch strips right sides together, lengthwise, in desired sequence, using ¼" (6 mm) seam allowances.

2) Place pieced strip across, rather than lengthwise, on ironing surface, to prevent distorting grainline during pressing. Press all the seam allowances in one direction, or, for a seam joining a light and a dark fabric, press seam allowances toward the dark fabric. Turn strip over, and press from the right side.

3a) Quilter's tool. Align 9" (23 cm) dotted line on Companion Angle with one long edge of the pieced strip; cut along angled edges of tool. Rotate tool and align with opposite raw edge to cut second triangle. Repeat to cut additional triangles.

3b) Template. Cut a 6⅞" (17.5 cm) square from cardboard or template material, and cut it in half diagonally to make triangle template. Align long edge of template with raw edge of pieced strip; mark along angled sides, using marking pencil. Rotate and realign template to mark second triangle. Repeat to mark additional triangles; cut triangles.

4) Cut 6⅞" (17.5 cm) squares from coordinating fabric. Layer squares, and cut in half diagonally to make triangles.

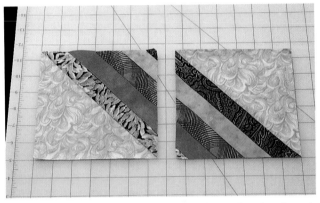

5) Align coordinating fabric triangle and strip-pieced triangle, right sides together; stitch on long edge, taking care not to stretch bias edges. Finger-press seam allowance toward darker fabric.

How to Sew a Diamond Design from Shadowed Square Quilt Blocks

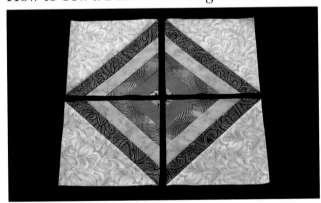

1) Follow steps 1 to 5, opposite; make four Shadowed Square blocks, using identical strip-pieced triangles. Arrange blocks to form a center diamond as shown.

2) Stitch blocks to form two rows; then stitch the rows together, finger-pressing seam allowances in opposite directions. Press block, pressing long seam allowances to one side.

Shadowed Square Pillows

For a quick quilting project, make a pillow using the Shadowed Square design on page 62. This pillow features a diamond design framed by a 3" (7.5 cm) coordinating border.

The pillow cover is designed to fit an 18" (46 cm) pillow form. For easy construction, the pillow cover back has an overlap closure, secured with hook and loop tape.

✂ Cutting Directions

For the pillow cover front, cut two 3½" × 12½" (9 × 31.8 cm) border strips and two 3½" × 18½" (9 × 47.3 cm) border strips. Also cut two 18½" × 13" (47.3 × 33 cm) rectangles, for the pillow cover back.

YOU WILL NEED

¼ yd. (0.25 m) each of four fabrics, for stripes of diamond.

⅝ yd. (0.6 m) fabric, for one stripe of diamond, border strips, and pillow back.

¼ yd. (0.25 m) fabric, for background.

⅝ yd. (0.6 m) muslin, for pillow lining.

Batting, about 20" (51 cm) square.

One 18" (46 cm) square pillow form.

2" (5 cm) strip of hook and loop tape, ¾" (2 cm) wide.

How to Sew a Shadowed Square Pillow

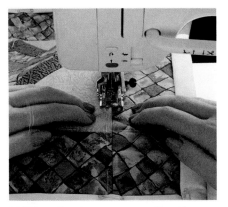

1) Cut and assemble four Shadowed Square blocks into diamond design as on pages 62 and 63. Stitch one short border strip to one side of block, right sides together and raw edges even. Press seam allowances toward border. Repeat on opposite side.

2) Stitch remaining border strips to the remaining sides of block. Press seam allowances toward the border. Press pieced pillow top.

3) Place batting over muslin. Center pieced pillow top, right side up, over batting; baste layers together (pages 16 and 17). Quilt the block, using the stitch-in-the-ditch method (pages 22 and 23).

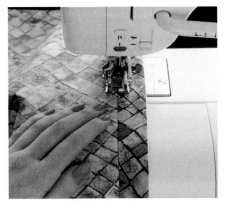

4) Press under 1" (2.5 cm) twice on one long edge of the rectangle for pillow back; stitch to make double-fold hem. Repeat for the remaining pillow back piece.

5) Position pillow back piece over the pillow front, right sides together, matching raw edges; hemmed edges of the back pieces overlap about 3" (7.5 cm) at center. Pin in place.

6) Stitch around pillow cover, ¼" (6 mm) from raw edges. Trim the batting ⅛" (3 mm) from seam. Trim muslin even with edges of pillow cover. Trim corners diagonally. Turn pillow right side out; press lightly.

7) Pin hook side of hook and loop tape to overlap, centering tape on hem; stitch around tape. Pin loop side of hook and loop tape to the underlap, directly under hook side of tape; stitch.

8) Insert the pillow form into pillow cover. Secure the hook and loop tape.

Shadowed Square Lap Quilts

Although this lap quilt appears intricate, it is actually simple to sew. It is made using the Shadowed Square design with a diagonal strip-pieced triangle (page 62) and several variations; half of each block is a plain fabric triangle. Easy strip-piecing techniques are used to assemble the pieced triangle designs.

Choose a printed fabric for the plain fabric triangles in each of the blocks. Then choose eight or more coordinating fabrics to use for the pieced triangles. Printed fabrics and fabrics with color gradations will make the finished quilt appear more intricate. The finished quilt with a double border measures about 44" × 56" (112 × 142 cm).

✂ Cutting Directions

In the directions that follow, cut the strips across the width of the fabric. Cut four 6⅞" (17.5 cm) strips from printed fabric; cut the strips to make twenty-four 6⅞" (17.5 cm) squares. Cut the squares diagonally as on page 63, step 4, to make 48 triangles. The fabric strips for the pieced triangles are cut on pages 68 to 70.

Cut five 1½" (3.8 cm) strips from inner border fabric. Cut five 3½" (9 cm) strips from outer border fabric. The strips will be cut to length for the inner and outer borders on page 71. Cut five 2½" (6.5 cm) strips from binding fabric.

YOU WILL NEED

1 yd. (0.95 m) printed fabric, for plain triangles.

⅓ yd. (0.32 m) each of eight or more coordinating fabrics, for pieced triangles.

⅓ yd. (0.32 m) fabric, for inner border.

⅔ yd. (0.63 m) fabric, for outer border.

½ yd. (0.5 m) fabric, for binding.

Batting, about 48" × 60" (122 × 152.5 cm) rectangle.

2⅔ yd. (2.48 m) fabric, for backing.

The Shadowed Square lap quilt (opposite) is made using the basic Shadowed Square block and several variations.

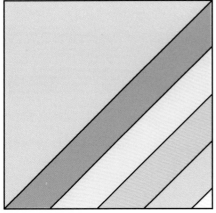

Block with diagonal strip-pieced triangle.

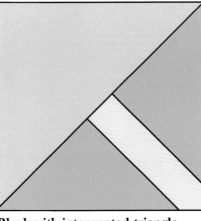

Block with interrupted triangle (version one).

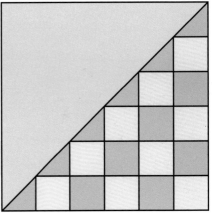

Block with 1" (2.5 cm) checkerboard triangle.

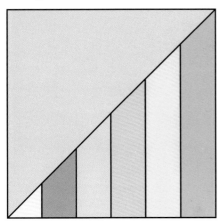

Block with vertical strip-pieced triangle.

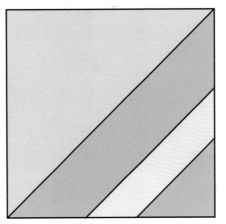

Block with interrupted triangle (version two).

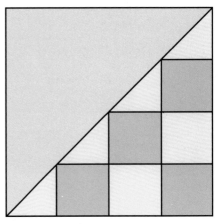

Block with 1½" (3.8 cm) checkerboard triangle.

How to Sew the Blocks for the Shadowed Square Lap Quilt

 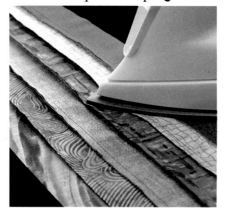 

Diagonal strip-pieced triangles. Cut and assemble eight strip-pieced triangles, as on pages 62 and 63, steps 1 to 3. Repeat to make eight additional triangles, using different fabrics or a different arrangement of the fabrics for the pieced strip.

Vertical strip-pieced triangles. 1) Cut one 1½" (3.8 cm) strip each from six fabrics. Stitch the strips together lengthwise in scant ¼" (6 mm) seams in the desired sequence. Press seam allowances in one direction.

2) Cut eight triangles from pieced strip as on page 63, step 3a or 3b; align short edge of template with the raw edge of pieced strip. Point of triangle extends slightly beyond one edge of pieced strip.

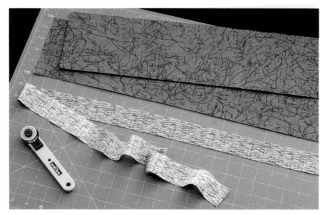 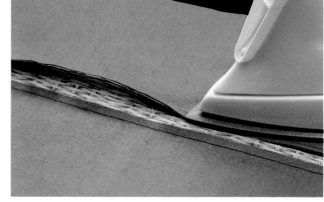

Interrupted triangles. 1) Cut one 5" (12.5 cm) strip from fabric; cut one 1½" (3.8) strip from a different fabric. Cut strips in half; discard one narrow strip.

2) Stitch a 5" (12.5 cm) strip to each side of narrow strip, in ¼" (6 mm) seams. Press seam allowances toward center strip.

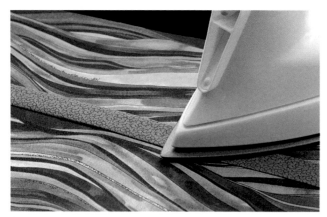 

3) Repeat steps 1 and 2 to make a second pieced strip, using different fabrics.

4) Mark four triangles on each pieced strip, using template or tool; vary the position of the template so the narrow fabric strip runs both horizontally and vertically across the triangles. Cut triangles.

How to Sew the Blocks for the Shadowed Square Lap Quilt

1" (2.5 cm) checkerboard triangles. 1) Cut two 1½" (3.8 cm) strips each from two contrasting fabrics; cut the strips in half. Stitch six strips together lengthwise, in scant ¼" (6 mm) seams, alternating fabrics. Press strip, pressing seam allowances in one direction.

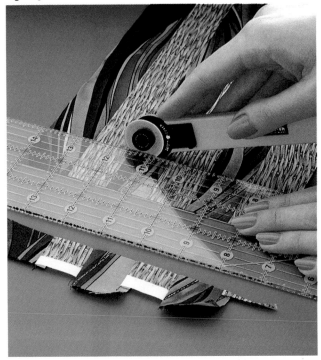

2) Repeat step 1, using different fabrics, to make a second pieced strip. Trim the short end of each strip at a 90° angle. Cut 1½" (3.8 cm) strips across each pieced fabric strip.

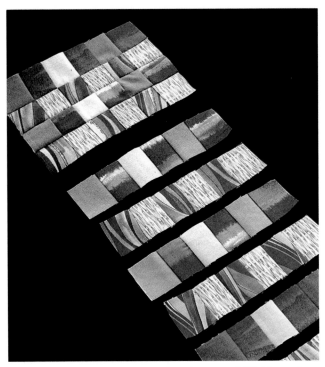

3) Stitch pieced strips together in scant ¼" (6 mm) seams, alternating them to form a checkerboard. Press seam allowances in one direction.

4) Mark eight triangles on strip, using a template or a tool, and aligning short edge of template with raw edge of pieced strip. Point of triangle extends slightly beyond pieced strip. Cut triangles.

(Continued on next page)

How to Sew the Blocks for the Shadowed Square Lap Quilt (continued)

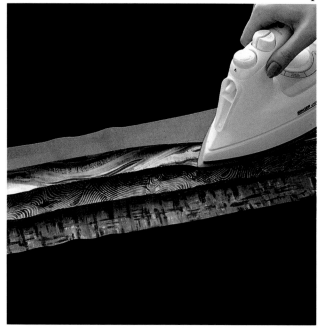

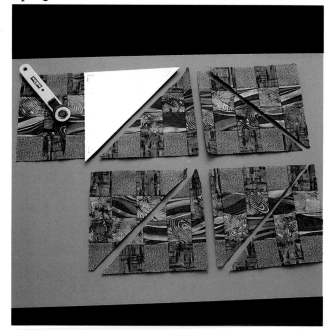

1½" (3.8 cm) checkerboard triangles. 1) Cut one 2" (5 cm) strip each from four fabrics. Stitch the strips together lengthwise in scant ¼" (6 mm) seams. Press seam allowances in one direction.

2) Cut 2" (5 cm) strips across pieced strip as on page 69, step 2. Reassemble strips, alternating fabrics to form a checkerboard. Cut eight triangles from strip as shown.

How to Assemble the Shadowed Square Lap Quilt

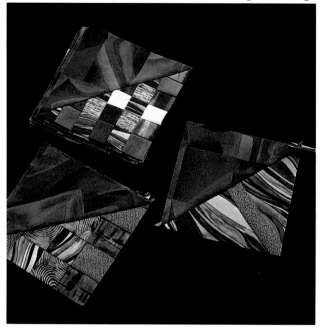

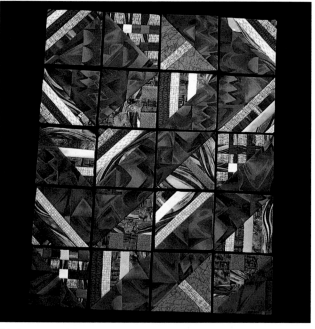

1) Place pieced triangle and plain fabric triangle right sides together; stitch on long edge, taking care not to stretch bias edges. Press the seam allowances toward plain triangle; trim points. Repeat to make 48 blocks.

2) Arrange blocks six across and eight down, rotating plain triangles to create a radiating diamond pattern. Stitch the blocks into rows; then stitch rows together, finger-pressing seam allowances in opposite directions. Press quilt top.

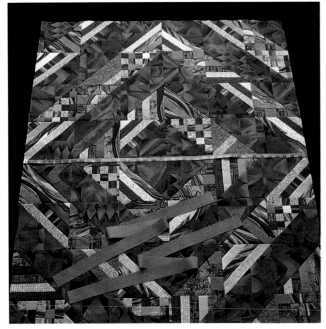

3) Measure the quilt top across the middle. Cut two inner border strips equal to this measurement, for upper and lower inner border.

4) Pin inner border strip to upper edge of quilt top at center and ends, right sides together; pin along length, easing in any fullness. Stitch; press the seam allowances toward inner border. Press from right side. Repeat at lower edge.

5) Piece remaining inner border strips as on page 26, step 2; trim seam allowances. Measure quilt top down the middle, including inner border strips. Cut two inner border strips for sides equal to this length. Pin and stitch the strips to sides of quilt top as in step 4.

6) Repeat steps 3 to 5 to apply the outer border. Cut backing fabric 4" (10 cm) wider and longer than quilt top, piecing as necessary.

7) Layer and baste the quilt as on pages 16 and 17. Quilt, using stitch-in-the-ditch method (pages 22 and 23). Apply the binding as on pages 25 to 27.

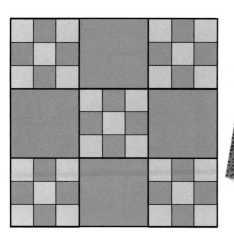

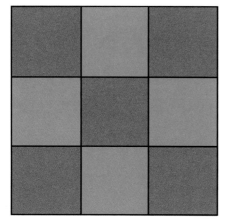

Nine-patch &
Double Nine-patch Designs

A Nine-patch quilt block, made from nine squares, is one of the most basic quilt blocks. The Double Nine-patch block alternates squares and checkerboard pieced squares. Each of the checkerboard squares is made from nine smaller squares.

Both styles of blocks are used in the sampler quilts on pages 87 and 89. One of these blocks is also used to make the sleeping bag on page 75, and the other is used for the coordinating tote bag on page 113.

The checkerboard squares used in the Double Nine-patch block are made using a strip-piecing method that lets you create intricate designs quickly without individually seaming small pieces of fabric.

The instructions that follow are for a 6" (15 cm) Nine-patch block and a 9" (23 cm) Double Nine-patch block. At least two fabrics are needed to make each quilt block.

How to Sew a Nine-patch Quilt Block

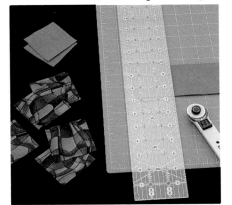

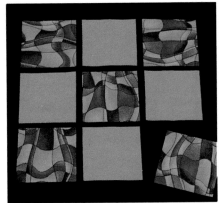

1) Cut five 2½" (6.5 cm) squares from Fabric A, and cut four 2½" (6.5 cm) squares from Fabric B.

2) Arrange the squares, alternating the fabrics, to form a nine-square checkerboard.

3) Assemble the quilt block, using chainstitching (page 15). Press the block.

How to Sew a Double Nine-patch Quilt Block

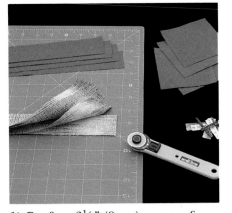

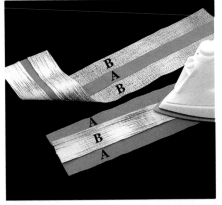

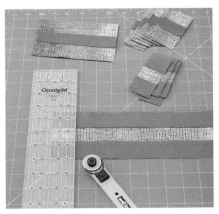

1) Cut four 3½" (9 cm) squares from Fabric A. Cut two 1½" (3.8 cm) strips across the width of both Fabric A and Fabric B; cut strips in half to make four strips of each.

2) Stitch one B-A-B unit and one A-B-A unit, right sides together. Discard remaining two strips. Press all of the seams toward the darker fabric.

3) Trim short end of each pieced strip at a 90° angle. Cut ten 1½" (3.8 cm) strips across B-A-B unit and five 1½" (3.8 cm) strips across A-B-A unit.

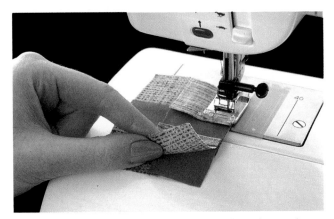

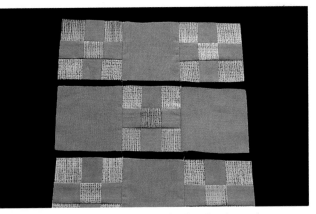

4) Stitch one B-A-B unit to one A-B-A unit on the long edges, right sides together. Then stitch B-A-B unit to the other long edge of A-B-A unit, right sides together, to form checkerboard. Repeat to make four more checkerboard units. Press the seam allowances toward the sides with the two darker squares.

5) Alternate plain squares with checkerboard squares to form the Double Nine-patch block. Assemble block, using chainstitching (page 15).

Nine-patch Sleeping Bags

Children will love snuggling down into their own patchwork sleeping bag, made with the Nine-patch design (page 72). A generous side opening makes it easy to get in and out of the sleeping bag.

Novelty printed fabrics, combined with a solid coordinating fabric, work well for the Nine-patch design in this project. The Nine-patch quilt blocks are separated by sashing with connecting squares. The connecting squares of the sashing can be cut from the primary fabric in the block to create a dominant diagonal effect.

Several timesaving techniques are used to construct the sleeping bag. The Nine-patch blocks on the front of the sleeping bag are stitched together quickly, using strip-piecing. Simple stitch-in-the-ditch quilting is used on the front of the sleeping bag; however, to save time and give a more intricate look to the piecing, the stitching is continued from block to block by stitching through the sashing. The back of the sleeping bag is constructed from one fabric piece and features channel quilting.

The instructions that follow are for a finished sleeping bag that measures about 34" × 58" (86.5 × 147 cm). A shorter bag, about 50" (127 cm) in length, can be made by eliminating one row of blocks and sashing. For convenience, the sleeping bag features ties at the lower edges so the bag may be rolled up and tied in a neat bundle.

✂ Cutting Directions

Cut the following strips across the width of the fabric: eleven 2½" (6.5 cm) strips from the primary fabric in the block and eight 2½" (6.5 cm) strips from the secondary fabric in the block. These pieces will be strip-pieced and cut to make the Nine-patch blocks.

Cut twelve 2½" (6.5 cm) strips from the sashing fabric; these will be cut to size for the sashing strips as on page 76, step 4. Cut two 2½" (6.5 cm) strips from the fabric for the connecting squares of the sashing; cut the strips to make forty 2½" (6.5 cm) squares.

Trim the width of the fabric for the back to 38" (96.5 cm). Cut two 38" × 62" (96.5 × 157.5 cm) pieces from the inner lining fabric. The sleeping bag lining is cut after the outer bag is constructed.

YOU WILL NEED

⅞ yd. (0.8 m) printed fabric, for primary fabric in block.

⅔ yd. (0.63 m) fabric, for secondary fabric in block.

1 yd. (0.95 m) fabric, for sashing.

¼ yd. (0.25 m) fabric, for connecting squares of sashing.

1¾ yd. (1.6 m) fabric, for back of sleeping bag.

3⅓ yd. (3.07 m) muslin, for inner lining.

3⅓ yd. (3.07 m) fabric, for lining.

Batting, two pieces about 38" × 62" (96.5 × 157.5 cm).

2⅝ yd. (2.4 m) grosgrain ribbon, ⅝" (1.5 cm) wide, for ties.

How to Sew a Nine-patch Sleeping Bag

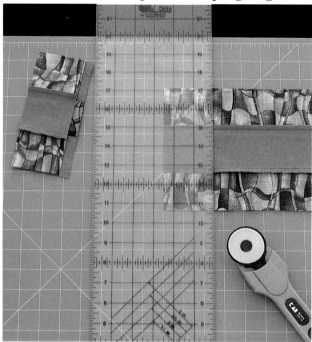

1) Stitch four B-A-B units and two A-B-A units, as for Double Nine-patch quilt block on page 73, step 2. Trim short end of each pieced unit at 90° angle. Cut 2½" (6.5 cm) strips across each pieced unit.

2) Stitch one B-A-B unit to one A-B-A unit on long edges, right sides together. Then stitch B-A-B unit to other long edge of A-B-A unit, right sides together, to form checkerboard. Press seam allowances toward the sides with the two darker squares.

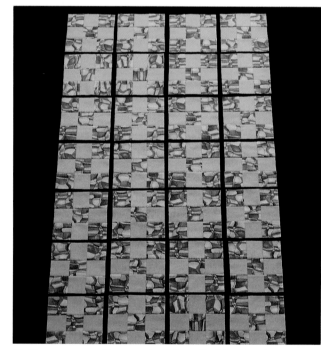

3) Repeat step 2 to make 28 quilt blocks. Arrange the blocks, four across and seven down.

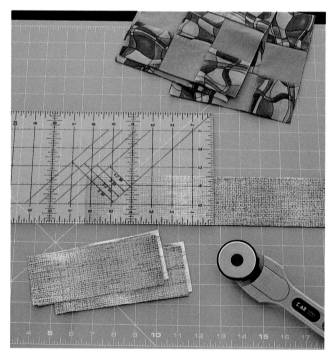

4) Measure sides of several quilt blocks to determine shortest measurement; using 2½" (6.5 cm) sashing fabric strips, cut 67 sashing strips to this length.

5) Attach sashing with connecting squares as on pages 34 and 35, steps 5 to 8.

6) Layer and baste the sleeping bag front, batting, and inner lining (pages 16 and 17).

7) Quilt, using stitch-in-the-ditch method (pages 22 and 23), stitching continuous rows through sashing.

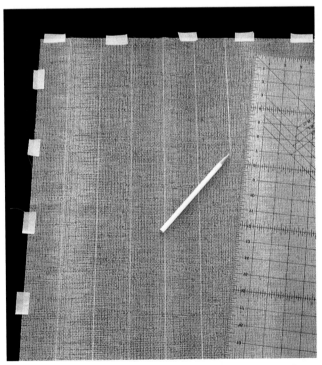

8) Trim batting and inner lining even with edge of the pieced top. Measure the front of the sleeping bag across and down the middle; record dimensions for use in step 14.

9) Tape the backing fabric to a hard, flat work surface, keeping fabric smooth and taut. Using a straightedge and quilting pencil, mark 2" (5 cm) parallel lines down length of fabric for backing. Remove tape.

(Continued on next page)

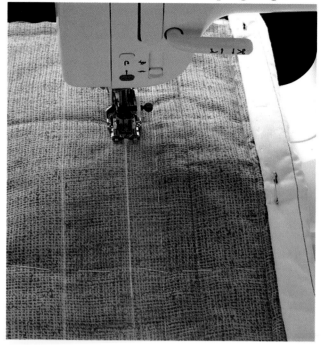

10) Layer and baste sleeping bag back, batting, and inner lining. Channel-quilt (pages 22 and 23) on the marked lines; reverse the direction of stitching every other line to avoid distorting fabric.

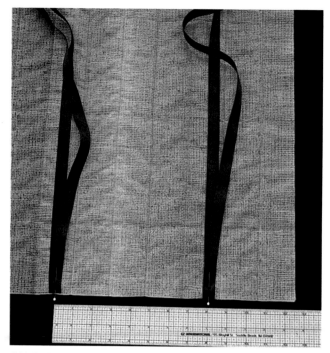

11) Trim back of sleeping bag to same size as front. Cut two 46" (117 cm) lengths of ribbon; fold each length in half, and pin to lower edge of sleeping bag back, 4½" (11.5 cm) and 12½" (31.8 cm) from one side. Stitch ribbon to bag, scant ¼" (6 mm) from raw edge.

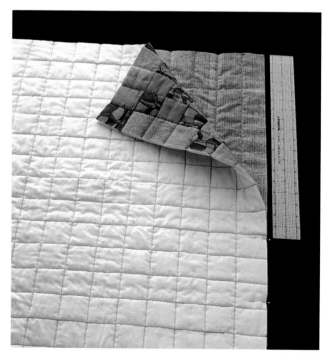

12) Pin the sleeping bag front to sleeping bag back, with right sides together and raw edges even. Pin-mark 18" (46 cm) from upper edge for opening on one side of sleeping bag.

13) Stitch around sides and bottom, backstitching at pin mark for opening. Clip the seam allowances at backstitching. Turn right side out.

14) Cut two lining pieces to dimensions of sleeping bag front; pin right sides together. Pin-mark side opening, and stitch as for outer section, leaving a 12" (30.5 cm) center opening on lower edge for turning; do not clip seam allowances at backstitching. Do not turn right side out.

15) Insert outer bag inside lining, right sides together; pin along side opening and upper edge, with the raw edges even. Stitch, beginning and ending at bottom of side opening.

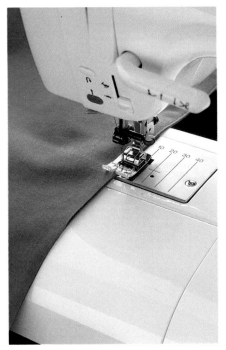

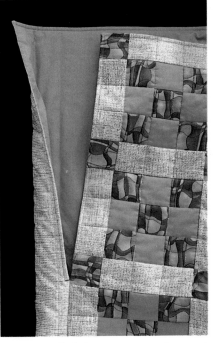

16) Turn the sleeping bag right side out through opening in bottom of lining. Edgestitch opening closed.

17) Insert lining inside the sleeping bag. Tack lining to bottom of outer bag at lower seam.

18) Press lightly on upper edge and side opening edges. Topstitch ¼" (6 mm) from upper and side edges. Stitch several times across bottom of side opening, to reinforce.

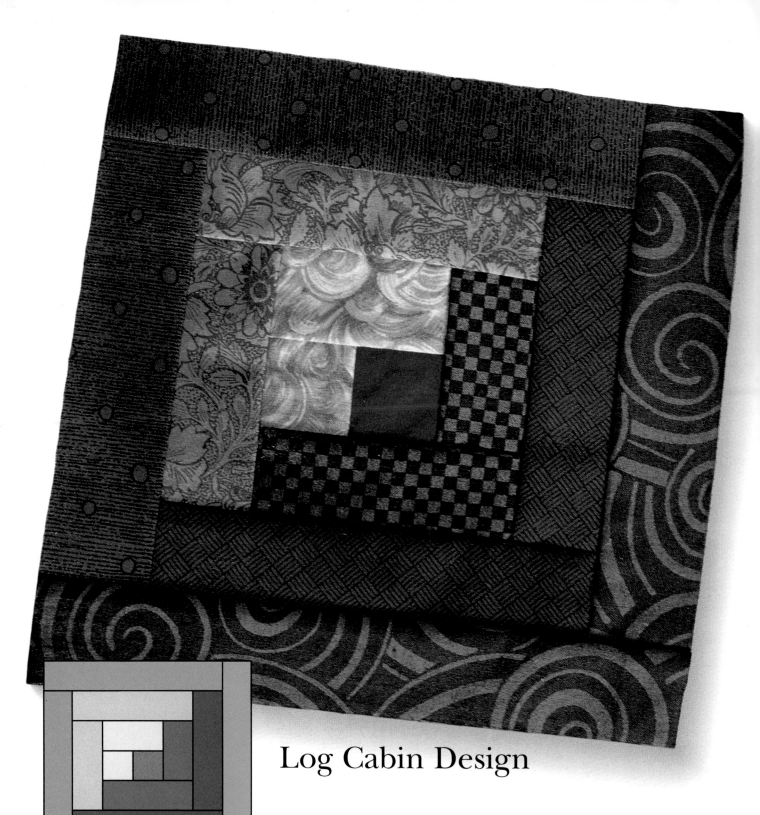

Log Cabin Design

Log Cabin remains one of the most popular traditional designs. The instructions that follow use chainstitching for quick and easy piecing of multiple blocks.

Choose three fabrics for each half of the block, and a fabric for the center square. Fabrics may graduate from light to dark, or from dark to light on each side of the center square, or they may be arranged in a random order.

The instructions that follow make a 7" (18 cm) finished block that is used in the sampler quilts (pages 87 and 89). A smaller Log Cabin block is used for the miniquilts (page 82).

How to Sew a Log Cabin Quilt Block

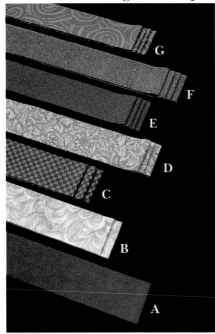

1) Cut 1½" (3.8 cm) strips across the width of seven different fabrics. Label strips from A to G, as shown.

2) Stitch Strips A and B, right sides together, along one long side. Press seam allowances away from strip A. Cut across the pieced strip at 1½" (3.8 cm) intervals.

3) Stitch pieced units to a second Strip B, using chainstitching (page 13) as shown.

4) Trim Strip B even with edges of pieced units. Press seam allowances away from center squares.

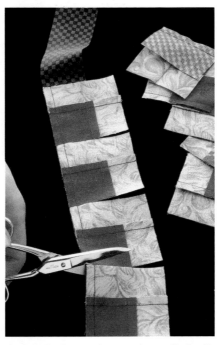

5) Stitch three-piece units to Strip C, using chainstitching; position units at 90° angle to most recent seam on side nearest center square. Trim Strip C even with edges of pieced units. Press seam allowances away from center squares.

6) Stitch four-piece units to a second Strip C, using chainstitching; position units at 90° angle to the most recent seam on side nearest center square. Continue in this manner, stitching two strips of each color to pieced units in sequence. Press the seam allowances away from center square.

Log Cabin Miniquilts

This trio of quilts, made using the Log Cabin design (page 80), creates a stunning wall display. The blocks in each quilt are arranged in a different way to create three different designs.

For a subtle blending of colors with a contemporary feel, make the blocks using hand-dyed fabrics as shown in the quilts opposite. These solid-colored fabrics are available in packets of six or eight fabrics and can be purchased from quilting stores and mail-order suppliers. Choose a printed fabric for the border, binding, and center square of the quilt blocks.

The quilts can also be made using a combination of printed fabrics. For best results, select fabrics for one half of the block that contrast with the fabrics for the other half. This emphasizes the design created by the block arrangement.

The quilts are made from 3½" (9 cm) blocks. Each of the finished quilts measures about 18" × 25" (46 × 63.5 cm). The yardages and the cutting instructions below are for a set of three quilts.

✂ Cutting Directions

Label the fabrics for the block design as on page 84, steps 1a or 1b. Cut the following strips across the width of the fabric: seven 1" (2.5 cm) strips each, from Fabrics B and C; eleven 1" (2.5 cm) strips each, from Fabrics D and E; and sixteen 1" (2.5 cm) strips each, from Fabrics F and G.

Cut two 1" (2.5 cm) strips from the fabric for the center squares of the blocks; these are Strips A.

Cut six 2½" (6.5 cm) strips from the fabric for the border; the strips will be cut to length as on page 84, steps 4 and 5.

YOU WILL NEED

½-yd. (0.5 m) bundle of six hand-dyed fabrics in a light to dark gradation; or ½ yd. (0.5 m) each of three light and three dark printed fabrics.

1 yd. (0.95 m) fabric, for borders and center square of each block.

½ yd. (0.5 m) fabric, for binding.

1⅞ yd. (1.75 m) fabric, for backing.

Batting, three pieces, about 22" × 29" (56 × 73.5 cm) each.

Log Cabin quilt blocks can be made from either solid-colored or printed fabrics and sewn into three design arrangements to make the miniquilts opposite.

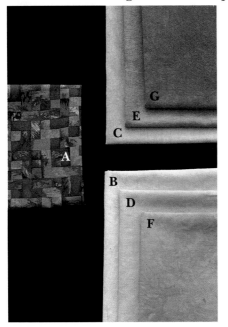

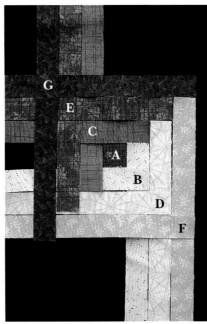

1a) Hand-dyed fabrics. Arrange and label six hand-dyed fabrics from B to G, graduating from dark to light and light to dark as indicated. Fabric for center square is Fabric A.

1b) Printed fabrics. Determine the arrangement of the fabrics, cutting narrow strips, if necessary; position three light fabrics on one half of the block and three dark fabrics on the other half. Label fabrics from A to G as indicated.

2) Assemble 72 Log Cabin blocks as on page 81, steps 2 to 6; in step 2, cut across pieced strip at 1" (2.5 cm) intervals.

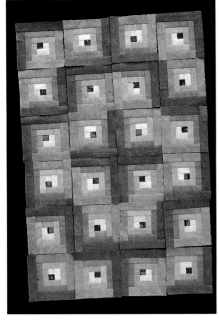

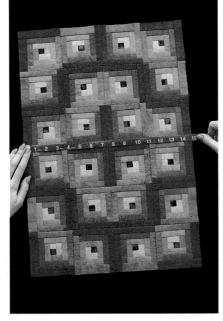

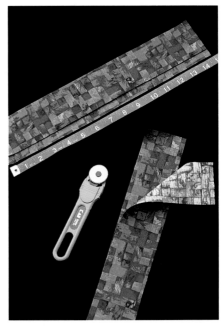

3) Arrange blocks four across and six down, as shown in the quilts on pages 82 and 83.

4) Stitch the blocks into rows; stitch rows together, finger-pressing seam allowances in opposite directions. Press quilt top. Measure each quilt top across the middle; determine shortest measurement.

5) Layer fabric strips for borders and cut six strips to measurement determined in step 4 for upper and lower borders; remainder of border strips will be trimmed to size for side borders on page 85, step 6.

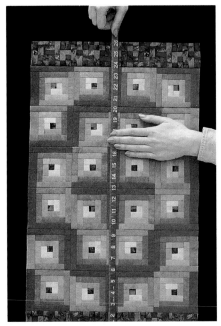

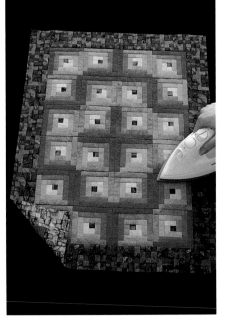

6) Stitch upper and lower border strips to each quilt top as on page 36, step 10. Measure each quilt top down the middle, including border strips; determine shortest measurement. From remaining border strips, cut six side borders to this length.

7) Stitch border strips to sides of each quilt top. Press seam allowances toward borders. Press quilt top.

8) Cut backing fabric for each quilt 4" (10 cm) wider and longer than quilt top. Layer and baste the quilt top, batting, and backing (pages 16 and 17).

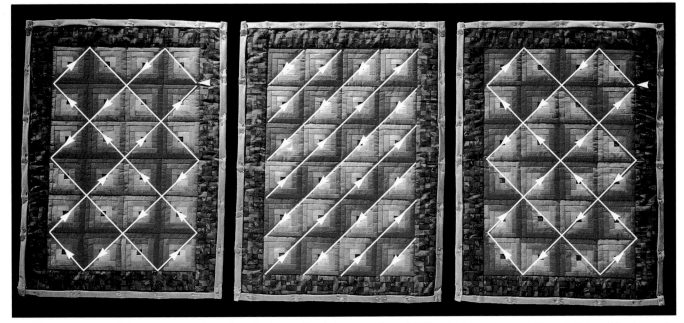

9) Quilt wall hangings, using stitch-in-the-ditch method (pages 22 and 23), stitching in seamlines joining blocks and borders. Stitch additional diagonal lines through centers of blocks to accentuate design as indicated by arrows. Apply binding to quilts as on pages 25 to 27. Attach fabric sleeve to each quilt (page 37).

Sampler Quilts

Sampler quilts are made from a variety of quilt blocks, united through color and size. The instructions that follow are for a 56" × 77" (142 × 195.5 cm) sampler quilt that can be used as a wall hanging, lap quilt, or twin-size bed quilt. Although the quilt may appear complex and intricate, it is easily assembled from the nine quilt blocks, plain fabric panels, quick-pieced checkerboards, and pieced-triangle strips.

The quilt is designed with four vertical columns that are separated by sashing strips. A narrow inner border frames the quilt, and Log Cabin blocks form a colorful outer border.

This sampler quilt is an attractive way to showcase a variety of quilting techniques. The example shown opposite has template quilting on the sashing strips, and the plain fabric blocks are embellished with free-motion stipple quilting, motif quilting, and template quilting.

Sampler quilts can be made using several fabrics, sometimes even as many as thirty. To simplify fabric selection, start with two or three multicolored fabrics to set the theme. Use the theme fabrics for the plain fabric panels; then incorporate them in some of the pieced blocks. The theme fabrics set the overall tone of the quilt. When choosing theme fabrics, think about scale. A larger print with many colors makes it easier to select the remaining fabrics.

Choose fabric colors with values that range from light to dark. Select a variety of fabrics, including solids, prints, checks, and stripes. You may want to keep swatches in a notebook and collect fabrics over a period of time. Multicolored prints work especially well when making the pieced checkerboard strips. Solid-colored fabrics are used for the sashing strips to separate and define the columns and the border of the quilt.

When piecing the quilt top, it is important to stitch scant ¼" (6 mm) seams. This allows for shrinkage resulting from multiple stitched seams and ensures that the pieced border will fit around the quilt top.

Sampler quilt (opposite) incorporates nine quilt block designs and a variety of quilting techniques.

✂ Cutting Directions

For Column One of the sampler quilt, cut one 7½" × 12½" (19.3 × 31.8 cm) rectangle and one 6½" × 12½" (16.3 × 31.8 cm) rectangle from theme fabric for the plain fabric panels.

For Column Two, cut one 6½" × 8½" (16.3 × 21.8 cm) rectangle, one 6½" × 9½" (16.3 × 24.3 cm) rectangle, and one 6½" × 11" (16.3 × 28 cm) rectangle from theme fabric for the plain fabric panels.

For Column Three, cut one 9½" × 10" (24.3 × 25.5 cm) rectangle and one 9½" × 11" (24.3 × 28 cm) rectangle from theme fabric for the plain fabric panels.

For Column Four, cut one 6½" × 10½" (16.3 × 27.8 cm) rectangle, and one 6½" × 12½" (16.3 × 31.8 cm) rectangle from theme fabric for the plain fabric panels.

For the pieced blocks and pieced strips, cut the fabrics as on pages 90 to 95.

For the vertical sashing strips, cut fabric strips across the width of the fabric. Cut two 3½" (9 cm) strips from first sashing fabric, to join Columns One and Two. Cut two 2½" (6.5 cm) strips from second sashing fabric, to join Columns Two and Three. Cut two 2½" (6.5 cm) strips from third sashing fabric, to join Columns Three and Four.

For the inner plain border, cut six 1½" (3.8 cm) strips across the width of the fabric. For the outer Log Cabin border, cut 1½" (3.8 cm) strips across the width of seven fabrics. Light-colored fabrics may be used for one half of the block and dark-colored fabrics for the other half. Cut the number of fabric strips as follows:
Fabric A, two strips for center squares;
Fabric B, four inner light strips;
Fabric C, six inner dark strips;
Fabric D, eight middle light strips;
Fabric E, ten middle dark strips;
Fabric F, eleven outer light strips; and
Fabric G, thirteen outer dark strips.

For the binding, cut seven 2½" (6.5 cm) strips.

YOU WILL NEED

Two or three multicolored theme fabrics.

Assorted fabrics, for pieced blocks and pieced strips.

¼ yd. (0.25 m) each of three fabrics, for vertical sashing strips.

⅓ yd. (0.32 m) fabric, for inner border.

Fabrics for Log Cabin border: ⅛ yd. (0.15 m) Fabric A, ¼ yd. (0.25 m) Fabric B, ⅜ yd. (0.35 m) Fabric C, ⅜ yd. (0.35 m) Fabric D, ½ yd. (0.5 m) Fabric E, ½ yd. (0.5 m) Fabric F, ⅝ yd. (0.6 m) Fabric G.

Batting, about 60" × 81" (152.5 × 206 cm).

3½ yd. (3.2 m) fabric, for backing.

⅝ yd. (0.6 m) fabric, for binding.

Diagram of the Sampler Quilt

Color-coded Identification Chart
for the Diagram of the Sampler Quilt

Log Cabin blocks	
Ohio Star blocks	
Pieced-triangle strips	
Checkerboard strips	
Theme fabrics (choose two or three)	
Shadowed Square blocks	
Drunkard's Path units	
Pieced Heart blocks	
Card Trick blocks	
Double Nine-patch block	
Spools block	
Nine-patch block	
Sashing strips (choose three)	
Inner border	
Binding	

How to Sew Column One of the Sampler Quilt

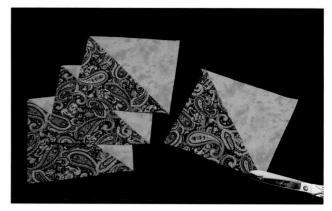

1) Sew one 12" (30.5 cm) block each of the following: Ohio Star (page 38), Drunkard's Path (page 44), and Shadowed Square (page 62). Set aside two of the remaining strip-pieced triangles from the Shadowed Square design for use in Column Two.

2) Cut two 6⅞" (17.5 cm) squares each from two fabrics for pieced-triangle strips. Layer squares and cut once diagonally. Stitch one triangle from each fabric, right sides together, along long edge. Finger-press seam allowances to one side; trim points. Repeat with remaining triangles to make four squares.

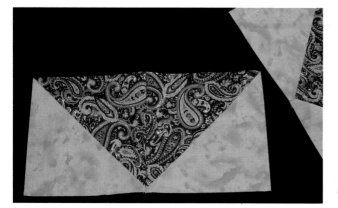

3) Stitch two pieced squares right sides together as shown, to make a pieced-triangle strip. Finger-press seam allowances to one side. Repeat to make a second pieced-triangle strip for Column Four; set aside.

4) Cut two 1½" × 20" (3.8 × 51 cm) strips each from two fabrics. Stitch strips together lengthwise, alternating fabrics, to make a 4½" × 20" (11.5 × 51 cm) pieced strip. Press seam allowances in one direction.

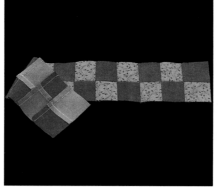

5) Trim short end of pieced strip at 90° angle. Cut twelve 1½" (3.8 cm) strips across the pieced strip. Stitch pieced strips together, alternating fabrics to make a 4½" × 12½" (11.5 × 31.8 cm) checkerboard strip.

6) Cut one 1½" × 20" (3.8 × 51 cm) strip from each of two fabrics; make a 2½" × 12½" (6.5 × 31.8 cm) checkerboard strip as in steps 4 and 5.

7) Stitch blocks, checkerboard strips, pieced-triangle strip, and the theme-fabric rectangles into a column as desired. Press the pieced column, pressing seam allowances in one direction.

How to Sew Column Two of the Sampler Quilt

1) Make one 6" (15 cm) Pieced Heart block (page 30); set aside the remaining heart units for use in Column Four. Using the strip-pieced triangles set aside from Column One, make two Shadowed Square blocks as on page 63, steps 4 and 5; in step 4, cut one 6⅞" (17.5 cm) square. Stitch blocks together as shown to make a vertical strip.

2) Cut one 7" (18 cm) square each from two fabrics. Using circle template with 5" (12.5 cm) diameter, cut one circle each from two fabrics, adding scant ¼" (6 mm) seam allowance. Continue to make a total of eight Drunkard's Path units as on page 45, steps 3 to 6.

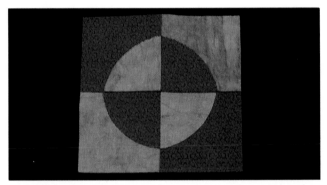

3) Arrange four Drunkard's Path units as shown. Stitch units together to form two rows; stitch rows together. Set aside remaining units for use in Column Four.

4) Cut three 1½" × 11" (3.8 × 28 cm) strips from each of two fabrics. Continue as on page 73, center, steps 2 and 3; in step 2, press seam allowances in one direction, and, in step 3, cut six strips across each pieced strip. Stitch strips together, alternating fabrics to make two 3½" × 6½" (9 × 16.3 cm) checkerboard strips.

5) Cut two 2⅞" (7.2 cm) squares from two fabrics for pieced-triangle strip; cut the squares in half once diagonally. Stitch one triangle from each fabric, right sides together, along long edge. Repeat with the remaining triangles to make three pieced-triangle squares.

6) Stitch the pieced-triangle squares together, side by side, to make a 2½" × 6½" (6.5 × 16.3 cm) strip. Finger-press seam allowances to one side.

7) Stitch blocks, checkerboard strips, pieced-triangle strip, and theme-fabric rectangles into a column as desired. Press the pieced column, pressing the seam allowances in one direction.

1) Make one 9" (23 cm) Ohio star block (page 38) and one 9" (23 cm) Card Trick block (page 50).

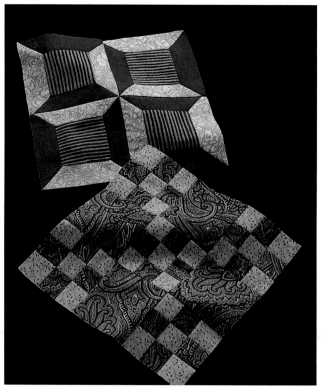

2) Make one 9" (23 cm) Spools block (page 56) and one Double Nine-patch block (page 72).

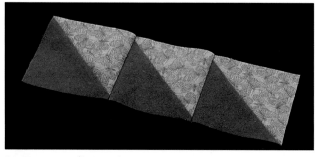

3) Cut two 3⅞" (9.7 cm) squares from each of two fabrics for pieced-triangle strip. Make a 3½" × 9½" (9 × 24.3 cm) strip as on page 91, steps 5 and 6; in step 5, omit reference to 2⅞" (7.2 cm) squares.

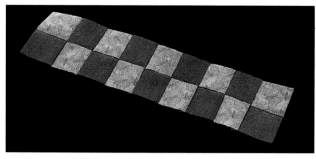

4) Cut one 1½" × 15½" (3.8 × 39.3 cm) strip each from two fabrics. Make 2½" × 9½" (6.5 × 24.3 cm) checkerboard strip as on page 90, steps 4 and 5; in step 5, cut nine strips across pieced strip.

5) Stitch blocks, checkerboard strip, pieced-triangle strip, and theme-fabric rectangles into a column as desired. Press pieced column, pressing seam allowances in one direction.

How to Sew Column Four of the Sampler Quilt

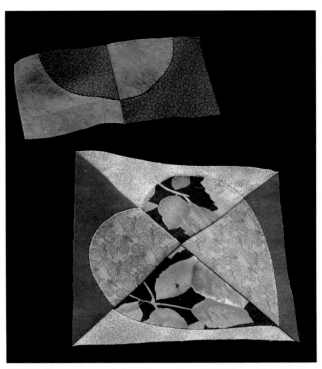

1) Make one 6" (15 cm) Card Trick block (page 50) and one 6" (15 cm) Nine-patch block (page 72).

2) Stitch two remaining Drunkard's Path units from Column Two together as shown to make a two-patch block; discard remaining units. Complete second 6" (15 cm) Pieced Heart block from units remaining from Column Two.

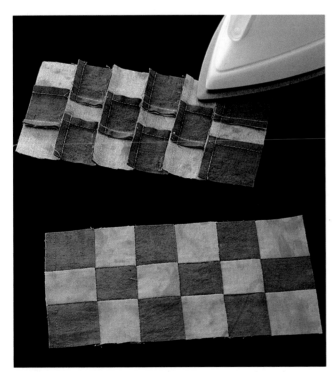

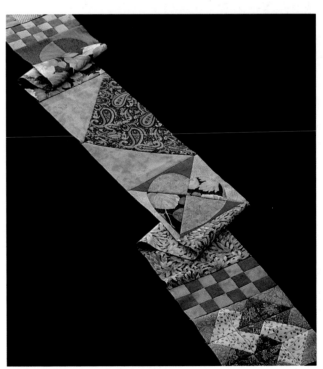

3) Make two 3½" × 6½" (9 × 16.3 cm) checkerboard strips as on page 91, step 4.

4) Stitch blocks, pieced-triangle strip, checkerboard strips, two-patch Drunkard's Path block, and theme-fabric rectangles into a column as desired. Press pieced column, pressing seam allowances in one direction. Assemble quilt as on pages 94 and 95.

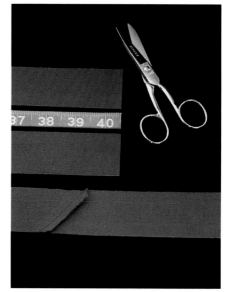

1) Stitch short ends of corresponding vertical sashing strips together as on page 26, step 2. Trim the seam allowances; finger-press to one side. Trim each sashing strip to measure 61½" (156.3 cm).

2) Mark centers of vertical sashing strips and columns. Pin one sashing strip to one column, right sides together, matching the centers and ends. Pin along length, easing in any excess fullness; stitch. Repeat to join all sashing strips and columns. Press the seam allowances toward sashing.

3) Stitch short ends of two strips for inner border together as on page 26, step 2. Trim the seam allowances; finger-press to one side. Repeat to make a second pieced strip. Trim pieced strips to 63½" (161.3 cm), for side strips of inner border. Trim remaining strips to 40½" (103 cm), for upper and lower strips of inner border.

4) Pin inner border strip to upper edge of the quilt top at the center and ends, right sides together; pin along length, easing in any fullness. Stitch; press the seam allowances toward the inner border. Repeat at lower edge.

5) Pin and stitch pieced strips to sides of quilt top as in step 4. Press seam allowances toward the inner border.

6) Assemble 34 Log Cabin blocks, as on page 81, steps 2 to 6. Stitch six Log Cabin blocks together for the upper border strip, placing the color values as shown in diagram on page 88. Finger-press the seam allowances to one side. Repeat to stitch strip for lower edge.

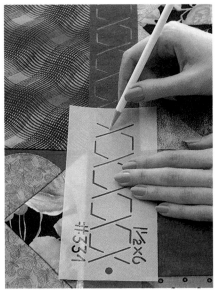

7) Pin the light-colored side of Log Cabin strip to upper edge of quilt top at center and ends, right sides together; pin along length, easing in any fullness. Stitch; press seam allowances toward the inner border. Repeat at lower edge.

8) Stitch 11 Log Cabin blocks together for the side border strip, placing the color values as shown in the diagram on page 88. Repeat for remaining side strip. Pin and stitch pieced strips to sides of quilt top as in step 7. Press the seam allowances toward the border.

9) Mark quilting lines for template quilting as desired (page 20). Cut backing 4" (10 cm) wider and longer than quilt top, piecing the fabric as necessary. Layer and baste quilt top, batting, and backing (pages 16 and 17).

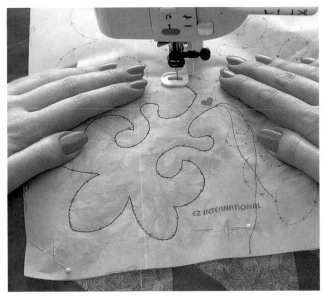

10) Quilt along sashing and inner border as on pages 22 and 23, using the stitch-in-the-ditch method; then complete free-motion and template quilting within the theme fabrics and sashing strips as on pages 22 to 24.

11) Stitch in the ditch along seams of pieced blocks as on pages 22 and 23. Stitch in the ditch between the Log Cabin blocks, and stitch through blocks diagonally in both directions, making an X; use continuous stitching, and pivot the stitching ¼" (6 mm) from raw edge at seams between blocks. Apply binding as on pages 25 to 27.

Quilted Garments & Accessories

Drunkard's Path Vests

Hand-dyed quilt fabrics and the raw edge appliqué technique are combined in this vest for color and texture. The vest is made using the Drunkard's Path design on page 44. As shown opposite and in the instructions that follow, a graduated effect is achieved by using fabrics that range from light to dark. Other color arrangements may be used for different effects.

Piece and quilt the outer fabric before cutting out the garment. For a lightweight vest without bulk, use a thin batting designed for quilted garments. Or use cotton flannel in place of batting. When using cotton flannel, be sure to prewash the fabric to help prevent shrinkage in the finished garment.

The Drunkard's Path units used in this project are constructed using a method similar to that on pages 44 and 45; however, it is not necessary to press under the edges of the circles. The circles are simply cut and stitched to the background square, allowing the raw edges to fray slightly.

Select a commercial pattern for a lined, loose-fitting vest. Avoid fitted vests, because the darts and the additional seams would interrupt the design of the pieced fabric.

✂ Cutting Directions

Cut two vest fronts and one vest back from lining, using the commercial pattern. The Drunkard's Path units for the pieced yardage are cut and assembled on pages 100 and 101. The vest fronts and vest back are cut from the pieced fabric and batting or flannel on page 101, step 10.

YOU WILL NEED

Commercial pattern, for lined, loose-fitting vest.

¼-yd. (0.25 m) bundle of hand-dyed fabrics, for circles; or ¼ yd. (0.25 m) each of several fabrics as desired.

Fabric for background, yardage indicated on pattern plus ¼ yd. (0.25 m).

Lining fabric; yardage indicated on pattern.

Thin batting, such as Thermore®, or prewashed cotton flannel.

Tear-away stabilizer.

How to Sew a Drunkard's Path Vest

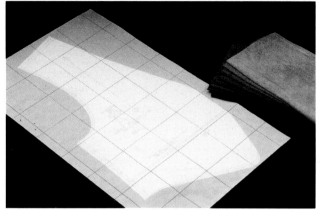

1) Measure vest fronts and vest back, and determine the number of 3" (7.5 cm) Drunkard's Path units that are needed for each piece; units extend beyond cutting lines. Estimate the number of units needed of each color; you need one circle for every four units.

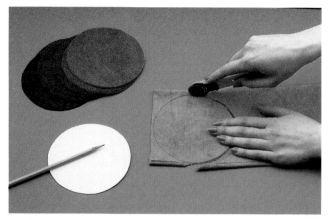

2) Cut a 5" (12.5 cm) circle from heavy cardboard or template material. Using template and pencil, trace template design onto fabric; cut out circles.

3) Cut 7" (18 cm) squares from background fabric, cutting one square for every four Drunkard's Path units. Center one fabric circle on background square, matching grainlines. Position tear-away stabilizer, cut larger than circle, on wrong side of background square; pin circle in place. Repeat for remaining circles.

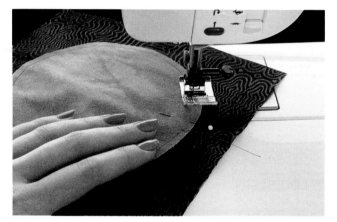

4) Stitch around fabric circle, ⅛" to ³⁄₁₆" (3 to 4.5 mm) from raw edge, using short stitch length. Repeat for remaining circles. Remove tear-away stabilizer, taking care not to distort stitches.

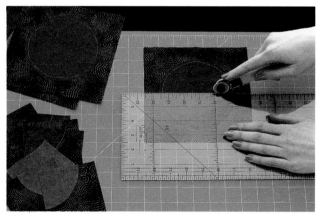

5) Cut through squares in both directions to make four Drunkard's Path units.

6) Arrange Drunkard's Path units for right and left vest front as shown, making sure the two sections are mirror images.

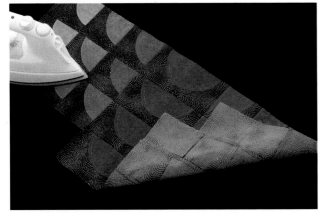

7) Stitch units into rows; then stitch the rows together, finger-pressing seam allowances in opposite directions. Press pieced sections.

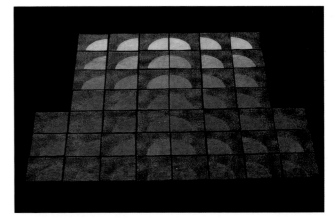

8) Arrange Drunkard's Path units for vest back as shown. Stitch the units into rows; then stitch the rows together, finger-pressing seam allowances in opposite directions. Press pieced section.

9) Cut batting to size for each pieced section. Place the pieced sections over batting; baste with thread or safety pins. Quilt, using stitch-in-the-ditch method (pages 22 and 23), in seamlines of pieced units.

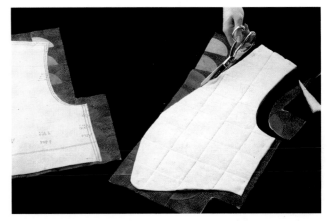

10) Cut two vest fronts and one vest back from quilted fabric sections, taking care to match quilted design at side seams. You may want to cut one vest front and turn the piece over, to use as the pattern for cutting the remaining vest front.

11) Complete vest, following pattern instructions; eliminate any interfacing from vest. Press vest from lining side to avoid shiny areas over seam allowances.

12) Brush edges of appliqués, using a stiff brush; this ravels the edges for more texture.

Pieced Vests with Triangle Squares

Triangle designs and a variety of quilting techniques give this vest its unique look. The left side of the vest features a pieced triangle strip. To balance the design, the right side of the vest has folded triangles of fabric, called prairie points, inserted into a diagonal seam. A pocket on the right side of the vest gives added detail. The lined vest is constructed using a low-loft batting. This provides the quilting dimension while adding minimal bulk.

Select a commercial pattern for a lined vest without darts. Because the fabric is quilted after the vest is constructed, choose a vest that is loose fitting; the quilting will cause the garment to shrink up in size slightly.

✂ Cutting Directions

Cut two vest fronts and one vest back each from the lining fabric and batting, using the commercial pattern pieces. The pieced outer vest is cut during construction.

For the pieced-triangle strip, cut one 3½" (9 cm) strip each from two or more fabrics, cutting across the width of the fabric; use at least one solid-colored fabric. Cut the strips to make 3½" (9 cm) squares; then cut the squares once diagonally to make triangles.

For the prarie points, cut three to five 4" (10 cm) squares from fabric.

YOU WILL NEED

Commercial pattern, for lined, loose-fitting vest.

Four or five coordinating prints, about ½ yd. (0.5 m) each.

Scraps of solid-colored fabrics, for pieced-triangle strip, prairie points, and trim on pocket.

Lining fabric, yardage as indicated on pattern.

Low-loft batting, yardage as indicated for lining.

Scrap of thin batting, such as Thermore®, or prewashed cotton flannel, for pocket batting.

How to Make the Pattern for a Pieced Vest with Triangle Squares

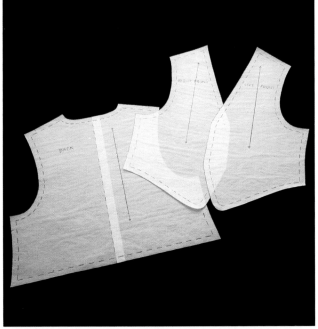

1) Trace pattern front, including seamlines on paper; turn pattern over, and repeat. Label pieces as right front and left front; mark grainlines. Trace pattern back, including seamlines on paper; turn the pattern over, and repeat. Tape the back pieces together along the center back seam. Label as pattern back. Cut the patterns on marked lines.

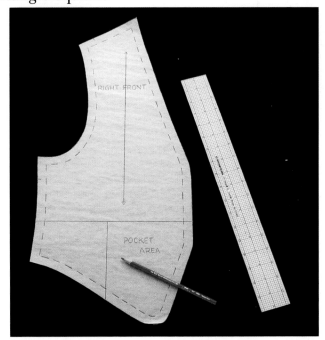

2) Mark a horizontal seamline on right front pattern, about 6" to 8" (15 to 20.5 cm) from the lower edge of the pattern; this line is also for the upper edge of the pocket. Mark a vertical line through the lower section; label lower right section as pocket area.

(Continued on next page)

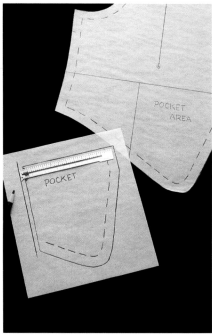

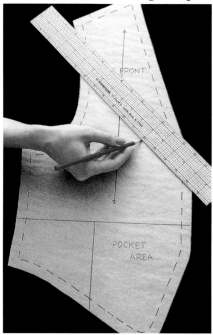

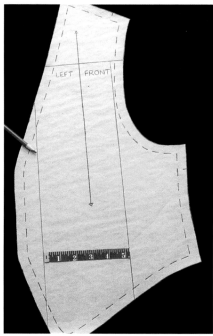

3) Trace the pocket area to make pocket pattern. Add ¼" (6 mm) seam allowance on inner edge as shown. Do not add seam allowance at upper edge. Mark grainline.

4) Mark a diagonal line through the upper right section, from edge of armhole to front edge; line at front edge should be at least ½" (1.3 cm) above the horizontal line. This is the seamline for inserting prairie points.

5) Mark a horizontal seamline on left front pattern, about 4" (10 cm) below shoulder seam. For the pieced-triangle strip, mark lower section with a vertical section, 5¼" (13.2 cm) wide, as shown; mark lines parallel to grainline.

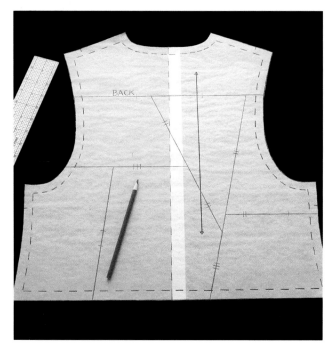

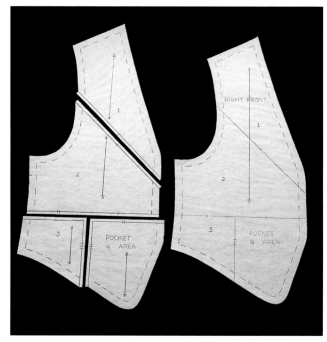

6) Mark a horizontal yoke seamline on vest back; mark line perpendicular to grainline. Divide lower section of pattern into three or more sections as desired, using straight or angled lines. Mark notches on all front and back pieces along new seamlines to indicate where vest sections are to be matched.

7) Trace the pattern sections for front and back on paper, adding ¼" (6 mm) seam allowances to inner seamlines. Mark grainlines on each section. Number the original pattern sections and traced sections to correspond. Cut pattern sections.

How to Sew a Pieced Vest with Triangle Squares

1) Make pattern, opposite. Set aside pattern sections for pocket and pieced-triangle strip. Using sections for vest fronts and vest back, cut one piece each from fabric as desired.

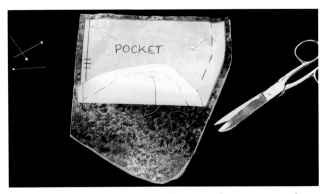

2) Cut one pocket piece each from the outer pocket fabric, thin batting or flannel, and the backing fabric, cutting pieces slightly larger than the pocket pattern. Layer fabrics; baste around the outer edges. Quilt as desired (pages 22 to 24). Cut pocket, using pattern. (Contrasting thread was used to show detail.)

3) Cut a 2½" (6.5 cm) bias fabric strip, with length of strip slightly longer than width of pocket. Press under ¼" (6 mm) on one long edge. Pin opposite edge of strip to upper edge of pocket, right sides together. Stitch ¼" (6 mm) seam.

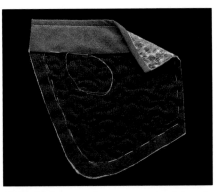

4) Fold bias strip to wrong side of pocket, creating ¼" (6 mm) binding on right side; stitch in the ditch on right side of pocket. Slipstitch folded edge of the strip to the wrong side of pocket.

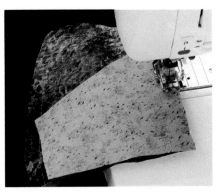

5) Pin pocket to the corresponding vest piece, labeled pocket area, matching raw edges at sides and lower edge; baste in place. Stitch pocket section to remaining lower section of right vest front.

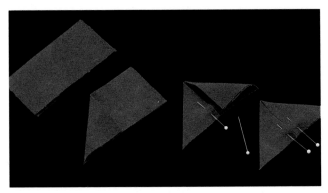

6) Fold each fabric square for prairie points in half lengthwise; press. Fold sides as shown, to make a triangle; press.

7) Position prairie points on upper section of right vest front, overlapping triangles as desired; folded edges may face either up or down. Pin triangles in place. Machine-baste in place a scant ¼" (6 mm) from raw edges.

(Continued on next page)

8) Stitch the upper right and middle right sections together, matching notches; press seam allowances to one side. Stitch upper pieced section to lower pieced section; press.

9) Stitch two different triangles for pieced-triangle strip, right sides together, along long edge; finger-press seam allowances to one side. Repeat to make about 14 pieced-triangle squares.

10) Arrange triangle squares, two across, in desired arrangement for the pieced-triangle strip. Make any additional triangle squares as necessary for required length or color arrangement. Stitch the squares into rows; then stitch rows together, finger-pressing seam allowances in opposite directions. Press.

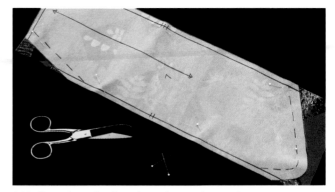

11) Cut pieced-triangle strip to size, using pattern set aside in step 1.

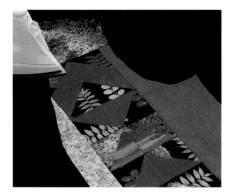

12) Stitch pieced-triangle strip to side sections of left front, in ¼" (6 mm) seams; press seam allowances away from the strip. Stitch lower pieced section to upper left section; press the seam allowances toward the shoulder seam.

13) Stitch together lower sections of vest back in ¼" (6 mm) seams, matching notches; press the seam allowances to one side. Stitch lower section to back yoke; press seam allowances toward yoke.

14) Place each outer vest piece over corresponding batting piece; pin in place, using safety pins. Baste batting to outer vest pieces, ½" (1.3 cm) from raw edges.

15) Stitch shoulder seams of front and back outer vest together; repeat for lining. Trim batting seam allowances of outer vest.

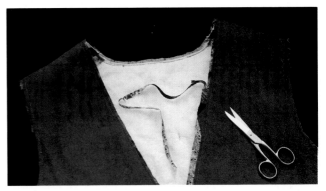

16) Pin the outer vest and lining right sides together, matching raw edges. Stitch around outer edges; do not stitch the side seams. Trim the batting and seam allowances.

17) Turn vest right side out through side openings of vest; lightly press edges. Pin-baste the layers together, using safety pins.

18) Quilt the vest (pages 22 to 24), changing quilting techniques as desired for each fabric section; do not extend stitching into seam allowances at side seams.

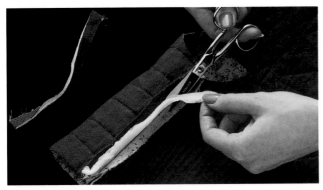

19) Stitch 5⁄8" (1.5 cm) side seams, with right sides together. Trim the seam allowances of the vest front to 1⁄8" (3 mm); trim the remaining batting seam allowance close to stitching.

20) Turn under 1⁄4" (6 mm) on the raw edges of the untrimmed seam allowances; pin, enclosing narrow trimmed edge. Hand-stitch folded edge to vest front lining. Hand-stitch the prairie points to the vest front, if desired.

Pieced-triangle Jackets

Make a quilted shawl-collar jacket using fabric pieced from equilateral triangles. A low-loft polyester batting is used to give the jacket loft and warmth. The outer edges of the jacket are trimmed with bias binding for contrast. Buttons are used to secure the layers together, adding extra detail and eliminating the need for machine quilting.

The 6" (15 cm) equilateral triangles can be cut quickly using a quilter's tool, such as the Easy Three™. Or they can be cut using a cardboard template. Piece the triangles randomly to make fabric yardage slightly larger than each pattern piece.

Choose a commercial pattern for a lined shawl-collar jacket that is loose fitting and has rounded lower corners at the center front. The loft of the batting will take up some of the design ease, making the jacket fit a little closer. Purchase yardage for the outer jacket to equal the total yardage indicated on the pattern plus ¾ yd. to 1 yd. (0.7 to 0.95 m) to allow for the seam allowances of the piecing. For example, if the yardage requirement is 4⅛ yd. (3.8 m), you may want to purchase 1 yd. (0.95 m) each of five different fabrics. For a coordinated look, purchase additional yardage of two of the fabrics to use for the jacket lining and binding.

To construct the jacket, the upper collar and front facing pieces are cut from the lining and stitched to the lining pieces to make a separate inner jacket. The batting is basted to the outer jacket only. When pinning the outer jacket pieces to the batting, you can prevent the batting from shifting by laying the batting on a carpeted floor or by taping the batting to the surface of a table. After basting, the inner jacket and outer jacket are stitched together and the outer edges are finished with bias binding.

✄ Cutting Directions

Cut 5¾" (14.5 cm) strips across the width of the fabrics for the outer jacket. Cut the strips into triangles, below, using the quilter's tool or template.

Adjust the pattern pieces as on page 110, steps 1 and 2. From the lining fabric, cut the front lining pieces, back lining pieces, sleeves, and the upper collar and front facing pieces.

For the binding, cut 3¼" (8.2 cm) bias strips.

YOU WILL NEED

Commercial pattern for shawl-collar jacket, selected according to the guidelines at left.

1 yd. (0.95 m) each of five or more fabrics, for pieced outer jacket.

Lining fabric, yardage as indicated on pattern; extra yardage may be required for cutting the upper collar and facing.

¾ yd. (0.7 m) fabric, for binding.

Low-loft polyester batting in twin bed size.

Buttons.

How to Cut Equilateral Triangles

Quilter's tool. Align Easy Three tool with fabric strip at the marking for 6" (15 cm) equilateral triangle; cut along angled edge of tool. Turn tool over, and realign with edge of fabric strip at marking for 6" (15 cm) triangle; cut along the angled edge. Repeat to cut triangles from all the fabric strips.

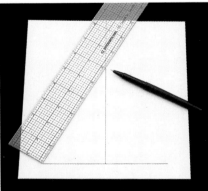

Template. 1) Mark a 6" (15 cm) line on cardboard or plastic template material. From center of this line, mark a perpendicular line. Align end of ruler to end of first line, and rotate ruler until 6" (15 cm) mark meets perpendicular line; draw line. Repeat for remaining side of triangle. Add ¼" (6 mm) seam allowances.

2) Cut template on marked lines. Align template with raw edges of fabric strips, allowing tip of triangle to extend on one side. Mark along angled sides, using marking pencil. Rotate and realign the template to mark the second triangle. Repeat to mark triangles on all the fabric strips. Cut on the marked lines.

How to Sew a Pieced-triangle Jacket

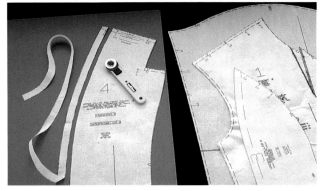

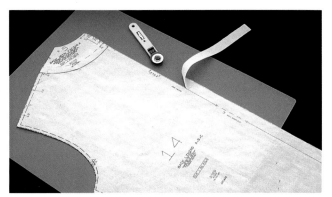

1) Trim seam allowances from center front of pattern for outer jacket, and on outer edges of the upper and undercollar pattern pieces. Trim the lower edge of front, back, and sleeve pattern pieces along foldlines for hems.

2) Align outer front pattern to front lining pattern. Trim lower edge of front lining pattern even with lower edge of outer front pattern. Repeat for outer back pattern and back lining pattern. Eliminate any center back pleat and any back neck facing on back lining pieces. Set aside sleeve lining pattern piece; sleeve lining is cut from outer sleeve pattern.

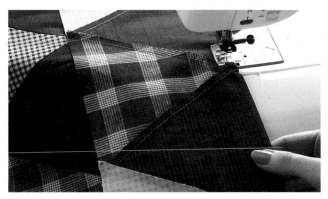

3) Stitch the triangles into rows, taking care not to stretch bias edges; position straight-of-grain edges of triangles along upper and lower edges of rows. Press seam allowances to one side. Rows for each garment section should be slightly wider than corresponding pattern piece.

4) Stitch rows together, aligning points; make sections of pieced fabric slightly longer than pattern pieces.

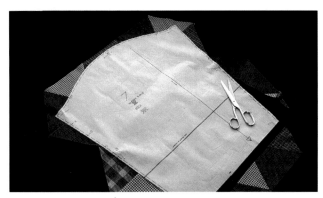

5) Cut jacket fronts, back, and sleeves from pieced fabric sections. Undercollar can be cut from pieced fabric or from plain fabric.

6) Position the outer jacket pieces and undercollar on batting; do not use upper collar and front facing pieces. Pin fabric to batting, using straight pins along edges of fabric and safety pins within the pieces. Cut batting even with edges of jacket pieces. Machine-baste layers together a scant ½" (1.3 cm) from raw edges.

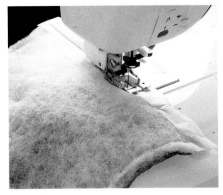

7) Assemble outer jacket, following pattern instructions; upper collar and front facing are stitched to lining in step 9. Place tissue paper strips against batting to prevent catching on presser foot and feed dogs. Trim batting from seam allowances.

8) Assemble and apply the patch pockets to jacket fronts, if included with pattern, following the pattern instructions; reinforce pocket piece with interfacing, if desired.

9) Staystitch the neck edge of back lining; clip to stitching. Stitch the upper collar and front facing to the front lining; then stitch to the back lining along the shoulder and neck seams, pivoting at the corners at neck edge.

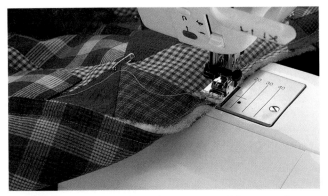

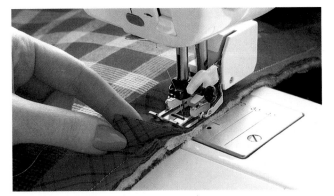

10) Place lining inside jacket, wrong sides together, aligning seams; pin along edges. Stitch scant ½" (1.3 cm) seams around outer edges of jacket and lower edges of sleeves.

11) Stitch binding strips together as on page 26, step 2; trim. Press binding in half, wrong sides together. Starting near side seam of jacket, stitch binding to jacket, with right sides together and raw edges even, ½" (1.3 cm) from raw edges; fold back ½" (1.3 cm) at beginning of strip, and overlap ends about ¾" (2 cm).

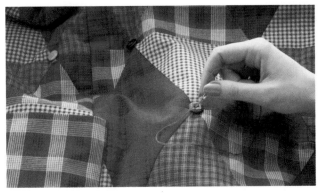

12) Wrap binding to inside of jacket as on page 27, step 8. Stitch in the ditch as on page 27, step 9, or hand-stitch binding in place. Apply binding to sleeves.

13) Quilt the jacket by securing buttons at points of triangles, stitching through all layers. Follow pattern directions for button and buttonhole closure.

Tote Bags

This generously sized tote bag is a handy carry-all for all ages. A center panel displays two quilt blocks on each side of the bag. To make a tote bag for carrying sewing supplies, use the Spools design on page 56 for the center insert. Or use the Double Nine-patch design on page 72 to make a tote bag that coordinates with the sleeping bag on page 75.

The lined bag has an inside pocket that is secured with hook and loop tape. Webbing is used to create sturdy handles for the bag and to trim the sides of the center panel.

For the efficient use of fabric, the side panels are cut on the crosswise grain. For this reason, select a nondirectional print.

✂ Cutting Directions

Cut two 6¾" × 39½" (17 × 100.3 cm) rectangles from the fabric for the side panels; also cut one 3½" × 9½" (9 × 24.3 cm) rectangle for the bottom of the center panel. From the lining fabric, cut one 22" × 39½" (56 × 100.3 cm) rectangle; also cut two 8½" (21.8 cm) squares, for the pocket.

112

YOU WILL NEED

½ yd. (0.5 m) fabric, for side panels and center bottom section of bag.

⅔ yd. (0.63 m) fabric, such as muslin, for inner lining.

1 yd. (0.95 m) lining fabric.

Batting, about 24" × 42" (61 × 107 cm).

3¼ yd. (3.0 m) webbing, 1" or 1¼" (2.5 or 3.2 cm) wide.

¼ yd. (0.25 m) hook and loop tape, ¾" (2 cm) wide.

Scraps of fabric, for quilt blocks.

How to Sew a Spools Tote Bag

1) Make four Spools blocks as on pages 56 to 58. Stitch lower edge of one block to the upper edge of second block, to make the center panel for front. Repeat for back center panel.

2) Pin front center panel to bottom piece, right sides together, matching 9½" (24.3 cm) edges; stitch ¼" (6 mm) seam. Repeat for back panel. Press the seam allowances toward bottom of bag.

(Continued on next page)

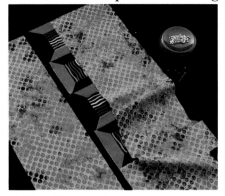

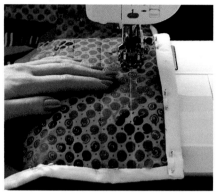

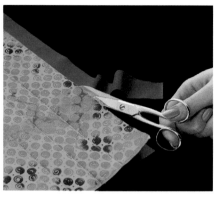

3) Pin side panels to center panel, with right sides together and raw edges even. Stitch scant ¼" (6 mm) seams. Press the seam allowances toward sides of bag.

4) Layer and baste the outer bag, batting, and inner lining (pages 16 and 17). Quilt (pages 22 to 24); use stitch-in-the-ditch method on quilt blocks and stipple quilting, channel quilting, or template quilting on side panels.

5) Trim the batting and inner lining even with edges of outer bag. Layer the quilted outer fabric over lining; trim lining to match.

6) Fold webbing in half; pin-mark. Stitch ends of webbing together in ½" (1.3 cm) seam; press open. Topstitch scant ¼" (6 mm) from seam on each side. Trim seam to ¼" (6 mm).

7) Glue-baste wrong side of strap to right side of bag, overlapping edge of webbing ⅛" (3 mm) over center panel; center the seam and the pin mark on strap on bottom of bag.

8) Topstitch along both sides of the webbing; begin and end stitching 1¼" (3.2 cm) from the upper edges of the bag.

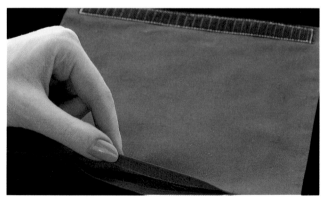

9) Fold bag in half crosswise, right sides together. Stitch ¼" (6 mm) seams on sides.

10) Stitch pocket pieces, right sides together, around all four sides, stitching ¼" (6 mm) from edges and leaving an opening along one side for turning. Turn pocket right side out. Cut 7¼" (18.7 cm) length of hook and loop tape. Center hook side of tape along upper edge of pocket; stitch in place.

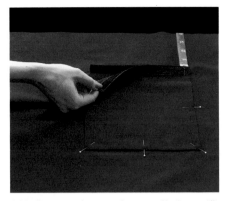

11) Center the pocket on lining, 4" (10 cm) from one short edge. Mark position for loop side of tape; stitch to lining. Reposition the pocket on lining; pin. Edgestitch around sides and lower edge.

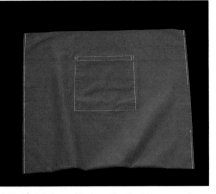

12) Fold bag lining in half crosswise, with right sides together. Stitch 1/4" (6 mm) seams on sides, leaving 6" (15 cm) opening in one seam.

13) Insert outer bag inside lining, right sides together. Pin along upper edges, matching side seams; finger-press seam allowances of bag and lining in opposite directions. Stitch 1/4" (6 mm) seam at upper edge; do not catch webbing in stitching.

14) Turn bag right side out through the opening in side seam of lining; machine-stitch opening closed. Press upper edge of bag.

15) Turn outer bag inside lining; align side seams. Mark a 3" (7.5 cm) line across corners. Stitch on line, through outer bag and lining.

16) Edgestitch along upper edge of bag. Secure the strap to top of bag as shown, stitching an X through all layers.

How to Sew a Double Nine-patch Tote Bag

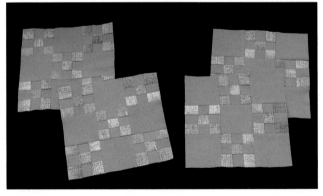

1) Make two Double Nine-patch blocks as on page 73. Make two more blocks, using four checkerboard squares and five plain squares in each block.

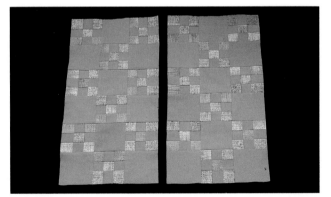

2) Stitch the blocks together as shown, to make front center panel and back center panel. Complete tote bag as on pages 113 to 115, steps 2 to 16.

Wallet-style Purses

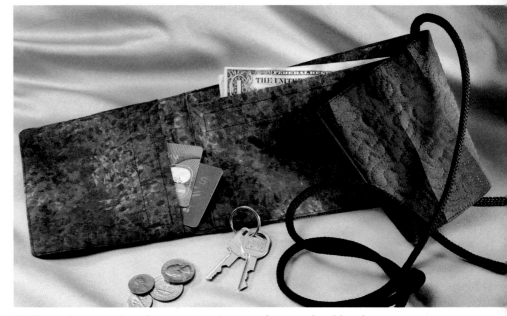

This quilted purse is divided into compartments like a wallet. It is constructed with three pockets for holding coins, credit cards, and a checkbook or currency. Each pocket is secured with hook and loop tape. The wallet becomes a shoulder bag with a length of decorative cording for the strap.

Wallet-style purse has three convenient pockets: a checkbook or currency pocket in the center, with coin and credit card pockets on the sides.

✂ Cutting Directions

Cut one 6½" × 19" (16.3 × 48.5 cm) rectangle from the outer fabric. Cut one 8" × 21" (20.5 × 53.5 cm) rectangle from the backing fabric.

Cut one 5½" (14 cm) strip from lining fabric. Cut the strip to make one 5" × 5½" (12.5 × 14 cm) rectangle and one 5½" × 7½" (14 × 19.3 cm) rectangle for the coin pocket. From the strip, also cut one 5½" × 6" (14 × 15 cm) rectangle and one 5½" × 9½" (14 × 24.3 cm) rectangle for the card pocket. Trim the remaining strip length to 5½" × 8½" (14 × 21.8 cm) for the currency pocket. Also cut one rectangle 8½" × 9½" (21.8 × 24.3 cm) for the currency pocket.

Cut three 4¼" (10.8 cm) lengths and one 7¼" (18.7 cm) length of hook and loop tape.

YOU WILL NEED

¼ yd. (0.25 m) outer fabric.

½ yd. (0.5 m) lining fabric.

Heavyweight fusible interfacing.

Batting, about 8" × 21" (20.5 × 53.5 cm).

¼ yd. (0.25 m) backing fabric, such as muslin.

⅝ yd. (0.6 m) hook and loop tape, ¾" (2 cm) wide.

1½ yd. (1.4 m) decorative cording, for shoulder strap.

How to Sew a Wallet-style Purse

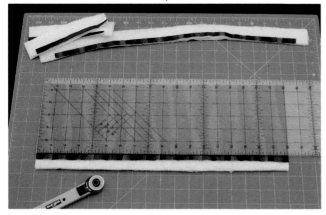

1) Layer outer fabric, batting, and backing; pin. Quilt as desired (pages 22 to 24). Trim the quilted piece to measure 5½" × 18" (14 × 46 cm).

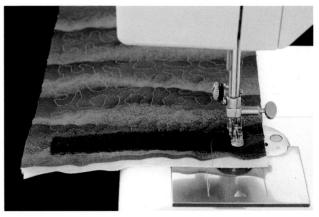

2) Center short length of loop tape on one short side of quilted rectangle, ½" (1.3 cm) from the edge; this end becomes underlap of purse. Edgestitch around all four sides of tape, using zipper foot.

(Continued on next page)

How to Sew a Wallet-style Purse (continued)

3) Fold the large rectangle for coin pocket in half crosswise, matching raw edges; press. Center a short length of hook tape ¼" (6 mm) from folded edge. Edgestitch around tape.

4) Turn the folded fabric piece over; center a short length of hook tape ½" (1.3 cm) from long raw edge. Edgestitch around tape.

5) Position folded fabric piece over remaining coin pocket piece as shown, aligning the raw edges. Mark position for loop tape on bottom piece.

6) Stitch loop tape in place. Baste the pocket pieces together, a scant ¼" (6 mm) from raw edges.

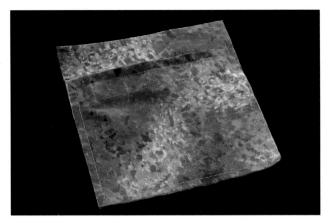

7) Assemble credit card pocket following steps 3, 5, and 6 for coin pocket.

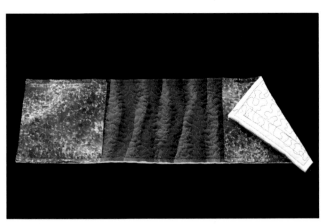

8) Place credit card pocket and outer purse piece, right sides together, at end of purse with loop tape; pin. Position coin pocket at opposite end of purse, right sides together; pin. Stitch ¼" (6 mm) from raw edges on all four sides.

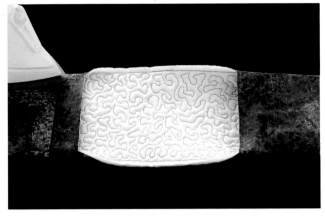

9) Trim corners diagonally. Turn purse right side out. Press lightly, pressing ¼" (6 mm) seam allowances at center area of purse to the inside.

10) Fold large rectangle for currency pocket in half lengthwise; press. Center long length of hook tape ¼" (6 mm) from folded edge; edgestitch around the tape. Align the folded piece to remaining currency pocket piece; mark position for loop tape. Continue as in step 6, opposite.

11) Place currency pocket over piece of heavyweight fusible interfacing, right sides together. Stitch around all sides ¼" (6 mm) from raw edges.

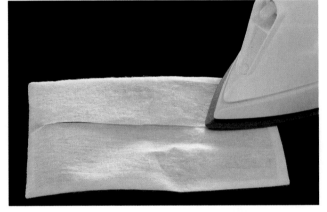

12) Trim corners. Cut a slit in interfacing; turn the pocket right side out through opening. Press pocket, fusing interfacing to back of pocket.

13) Center currency pocket on inside of purse, with ends of pocket about ⅞" (2.2 cm) from folded edge of adjacent pockets. Insert ends of cording under currency pocket, at upper edge of purse, as shown; glue-baste in place.

14) Edgestitch around currency pocket. Turn to right side; edgestitch the front flaps, reinforcing the stitching at cording.

Pieced Heart Baby Buntings

This quilted bunting makes a perfect baby gift. It has a pieced inset featuring the Pieced Heart design (pages 30 and 31). Narrow edging strips add definition to each side of the band. Stitch-in-the-ditch quilting is used on the Pieced Heart band. The upper and lower sections of the bunting can be quilted, using one of the other quilting techniques on pages 22 to 24, including channel quilting, stipple quilting, or motif quilting.

The lined bunting has a center front zipper opening for convenience. Boxed corners at the bottom give dimension to the bag, allowing room for the baby to move. The finished bunting is about 18" (46 cm) wide and 27" (68.5 cm) long, and can accommodate a blanket, if additional warmth is desired. A smaller bunting can be made by using five quilt blocks and trimming 2" (5 cm) from the length of the bunting.

✂ Cutting Directions

From the outer fabric, cut one 5½" (14 cm) strip for the upper section of the bunting and one 16½" (41.8 cm) strip for the lower section, cutting across the width of the fabric. The sections are cut to the correct widths on page 122.

For the border, cut two 1" (2.5 cm) strips each from two fabrics; the strips must be at least 39" (99 cm) long.

YOU WILL NEED

¾ yd. (0.7 m) outer fabric, for upper and lower sections of bunting.

Fabric scraps, for Pieced Heart blocks and border strips; or ¼ yd. (0.25 m) each of at least two fabrics for hearts and two fabrics for background.

1 yd. (0.95 m) backing fabric.

1 yd. (0.95 m) lining fabric.

Low-loft batting, about 34" × 42" (86.5 × 107 cm).

18" (46 cm) zipper.

How to Sew a Pieced Heart Baby Bunting

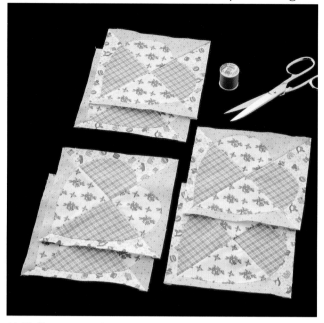

1) **Follow** steps 1 to 8 on page 31 to make two Pieced Heart quilt blocks. Repeat twice, using different fabrics, if desired, to make six blocks.

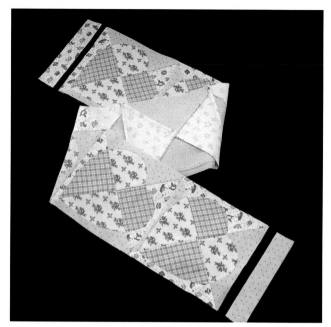

2) **Arrange** blocks into a horizontal row as desired; stitch blocks together along the sides in 1/4" (6 mm) seams. Cut two 1 1/4" × 6 1/2" (3.2 × 16.3 cm) strips for the extensions and facings at the ends of pieced band; cut strips from background fabrics that match the block fabrics at the ends of the band.

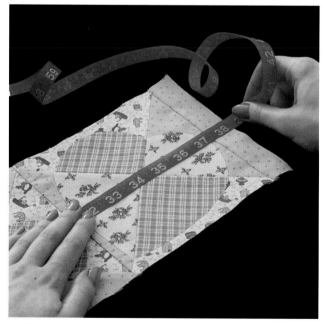

3) **Stitch** strips for extensions and facings to ends of band in 1/4" (6 mm) seams. Press seam allowances toward the facing. Extension and facing strips extend the band to allow for a 3/4" (2 cm) seam allowance at center front of the bunting. Measure width of band, including extensions and facings.

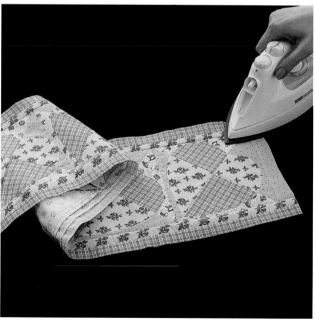

4) **Trim** upper and lower sections of bunting and border strips to measurement determined in step 3. Stitch two border strips together lengthwise, right sides together, in 1/4" (6 mm) seam. Stitch pieced strip to upper edge of pieced band. Repeat at lower edge of band with the remaining two strips. Press the seam allowances away from Pieced Heart blocks.

5) Stitch pieced band to upper and lower bunting sections in ¼" (6 mm) seams. Press seam allowances toward band. Mark the quilting design lines on upper and lower sections of the bunting, if necessary, as on page 20.

6) Cut backing 4" (10 cm) wider and longer than quilt top. Layer and baste the quilt top, batting, and backing (pages 16 and 17). Quilt (pages 22 to 24); use stitch-in-the-ditch method on the pieced band and channel quilting, stipple quilting, or motif quilting on upper and lower sections.

7) Trim batting and backing fabric even with edges of quilt top. Measure length and width of quilt top; cut lining fabric to this size.

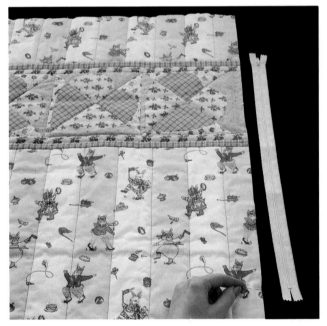

8) Pin-mark position of zipper bottom stop on center front seam allowance, with zipper tab at upper edge of pieced band. Pin quilt top, right sides together, at the center front. Machine-baste center front seam the length of the zipper, ¾" (2 cm) from edge; stitch the seam below zipper, using regular stitch length.

(Continued on next page)

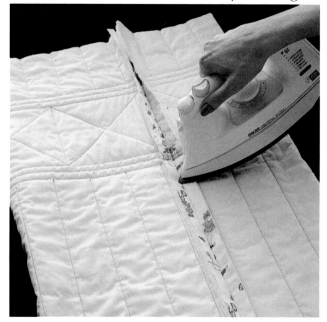

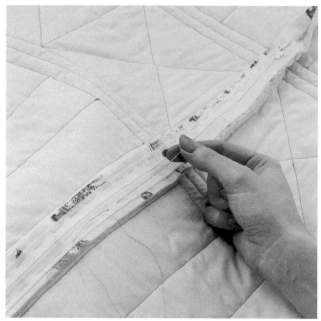

9) Press the seam allowances to flatten batting. Press seam open, using tip of iron.

10) Apply glue stick lightly to the face side of zipper. Place zipper facedown on seam, aligning zipper coil to seamline; press down to secure. Hand-baste zipper tape to seam allowances through all layers.

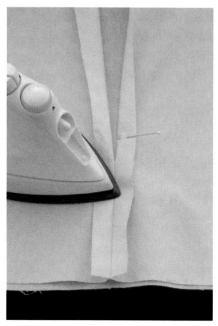

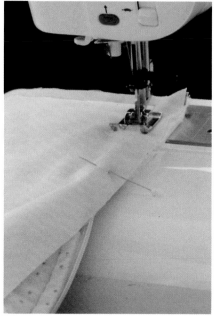

11) Turn bunting right side out; pin-mark bottom stop of zipper. Using zipper foot, topstitch around zipper about ¼" (6 mm) from seamline; in the pieced section, stitch in the ditch of the seam along the facing strip. In the lower section, center ½" (1.3 cm) transparent tape over seamline to use as a guide.

12) Fold lining right sides together; pin in place, and mark zipper stop. Stitch ¾" (2 cm) center front seam, from the lower edge to 1" (2.5 cm) below zipper stop. Press seam open.

13) Pin lining to outer fabric, right sides together, at upper edge and front edges. Stitch a ¼" (6 mm) seam allowance at upper edge and ¾" (2 cm) seam allowance at front edges; start and end stitching about 1" (2.5 cm) above zipper.

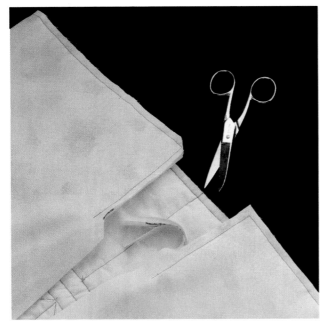

14) Trim corners diagonally; trim and taper seam allowances at front edges.

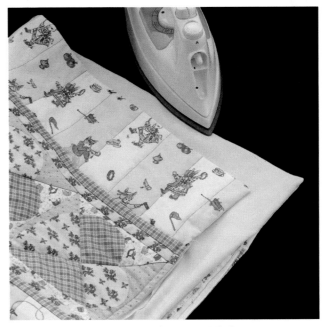

15) Turn bunting right side out. Lightly press upper and front edges.

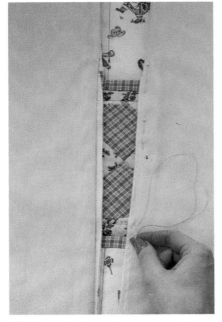

16) Turn the bunting wrong side out. Smooth the lining into position, matching center front seams; pin along lower edge. Fold under seam allowances of lining at center front; pin. Slipstitch lining to zipper tape.

17) Stitch a ¼" (6 mm) seam at the lower edge; finish seam, using a zigzag or overlock stitch. Stitch about 4½" (11.5 cm) across the corners through all the layers as shown, to make boxed corners. Turn bunting right side out.

18) Topstitch upper edge and front edges, overlapping stitches at upper edge of zipper.

Index

Cy DeCosse Incorporated offers a variety of how-to books. For information write:
    Cy DeCosse Subscriber Books
    5900 Green Oak Drive
    Minnetonka, MN 55343